A Flawed Freedom

T0385492

A Flawed Freedom

Rethinking Southern African Liberation

John S. Saul

PlutoPress
www.plutobooks.com

Between the Lines
TORONTO

First published in the UK in 2014 by Pluto Press
345 Archway Road, London N6 5AA
www.plutobooks.com

Distributed in the United States of America exclusively by
Palgrave Macmillan, a division of St. Martin's Press LLC,
175 Fifth Avenue, New York, NY 10010

First published in Canada in 2014 by Between the Lines
401 Richmond Street West, Studio 277, Toronto, Ontario M5V 3A8 Canada
1-800-718-7201
www.btlbooks.com

British Library Cataloguing in Publication Data
A catalogue record for this book is available from the British Library

ISBN 978 0 7453 3480 6   Hardback
ISBN 978 0 7453 3479 0   Pluto Press paperback
ISBN 978 1 77113 150 6   Between the Lines paperback
ISBN 978 1 7837 1141 3   Pluto Press PDF eBook
ISBN 978 1 77113 152 0   Between the Lines PDF eBook
ISBN 978 1 7837 1143 7   Kindle eBook
ISBN 978 1 7837 1142 0   Pluto Press epub
ISBN 978 1 77113 151 3   Between the Lines epub

Library of Congress Cataloging in Publication Data applied for

Library and Archives Canada Cataloguing in Publication
Saul, John S., 1938-, author
    A flawed freedom : rethinking Southern African liberation / John S. Saul.
Includes bibliographical references and index.
Issued in print and electronic formats.
ISBN 978-1-77113-150-6 (pbk.).–ISBN 978-1-77113-151-3 (epub).–
ISBN 978-1-77113-152-0 (pdf)
    1. Post-apartheid era–Africa, Southern. 2. Africa, Southern–
Social conditions–1994-. 3. Africa, Southern–Economic conditions–
1994-. 4. Africa, Southern–Politics and government–1994-. I. Title.
DT1182.S38 2014   968.0009'051   C2013-907910-6
                                           C2013-907911-4

Between the Lines gratefully acknowledges assistance for its publishing activities from
the Canada Council for the Arts, the Ontario Arts Council, the Government of Ontario
through the Ontario Book Publishers Tax Credit program, and the Government of Canada
through the Canada Book Fund.

10 9 8 7 6 5 4 3 2 1

Simultaneously printed digitally by CPI Antony Rowe, Chippenham, UK
and Edwards Bros in the United States of America

for Ruth First
activist, scholar and friend
a martyr in the struggle to achieve freedom
in her own country

Contents

Contents

"Globalization Made Me Do It" vs. "The Struggle Continues"

This book caps a series of volumes that I have written over the past decade, volumes focussing on the grim reality of recolonization (by an "Empire of Capital") found to be now gripping much of the "Global South" (not least the southern Africa region) and charting my own attempts both to analyze and to theorize this reality.[1] In the present volume I seek explicitly to sum

---

1   The first such book – now almost a decade old – was John S. Saul, *The Next Liberation Struggle: Capitalism, Socialism and Democracy in Southern Africa*, co-published in 2005 (in Canada, the United States, the UK and South Africa) by Between the Lines, Monthly Review Press, Merlin Press and the University of KwaZulu-Natal Press. There followed three shorter volumes – *Development After Globalization* (2006), *Empire and Decolonization* (2007) and *Liberation Lite* (2011) that were, like the present book, first published by Asad Zaidi and his Three Essays Collective in Delhi and that were also co-published, variously, by a range of additional publishers both in South Africa and in the North Atlantic world (the University of KwaZulu/Natal Press, Wits University Press, Zed Press, Merlin Press, and African World Press). Such writing was complemented both by an autobiographical volume on related subjects (Saul, *Revolutionary Traveller: Freeze-Frames from a Life* [Winnipeg: Arbeiter Ring Publishers. 2009]) and by a book recounting the history of South Africa, one co-authored with Patrick Bond and entitled *South Africa – The Present as History: From Mrs. Ples to Mandela and Marikana* (Oxford: James Currey, 2014). On my use of the concepts both of "recolonization" and of "the Empire of Capital" see, in particular, *Decolonization and Empire*, cited above, and especially its "Introduction."

up and to synthesize such findings as indices of the "flawed freedom" that the southern African region has realized, focussing ever more sharply on that region while also continuing to read off more general lessons from that region's specific experiences.

One initial point needs underscoring, however. This is that I continue to write of what I term to have been "the thirty years war for southern African liberation" (from 1960 to 1990) as an event of singular and positive significance.[2] For it is impossible to gainsay the importance, throughout the region, of the diverse "liberation struggles" themselves – struggles realized, principally, in Angola, Mozambique, Zimbabwe, Namibia and South Africa that contributed to the overthrow of the grotesque white-racist dictatorships that had been harboured in southern Africa well into the second half of the twentieth century. Here would seem to be a glass of freedom – and a struggle to realize it – that is at least "half-full," as the popular phrase goes.

It is not difficult, however, to see that very same glass of southern African freedom as being, simultaneously, "half-empty." Indeed, in this book I will also write quite critically of the initial wave of southern African "decolonization" and question pointedly just how much "freedom" it actually did, in the end, serve to establish. For it can be argued perfectly plausibly that the success of "liberation," as cast simply in national and racial terms, has made something of a mockery of the decades of liberation struggle that had once seemed to promise so much to the people in that particular corner of the world – and this in terms of the lack of transcendence, throughout the region, of class-based inequalities of power and circumstance, of any effective challenge to the continuing sway of gender-defined oppression and racial privilege, and of any resistance to

2   Some would take this "thirty years war" as continuing until 1994, finally to culminate in the accession to power of an ANC government in South Africa in that year. Indeed, I am currently preparing a comprehensive history of the war for Cambridge University Press to be published under the title *The Thirty Years War for Southern African Liberation, 1960-1994*.

the disempowerment of the region's vast majority of rightful claimants to democratic voice. Simply put, it remains the case that there has been virtually no on-going challenge to the continuing grip of global capitalism upon any of the ostensibly "liberated" countries of the region. Nor any effective challenge to those smug post-colonial regimes in the "new" southern Africa, regimes that continue to nurture inequalities and substantive underdevelopment there. For these reasons I feel constrained to underscore, as stated above, the existence of a distinct process of recolonization in southern Africa – a result that, in its present scarring of the region in question, has been both anti-climactic in its essence and humanly damaging in the extreme.

"Half-full" and "half-empty," then: the fact is that both terms of this paradox are true. What this leaves us with is a successful regional liberation struggle that has also been something of a failure, one capable of producing merely the "flawed freedom" of this book's title. At the same time, it is important, as we near the mid-point of the second decade of the twenty-first century, to focus on the concrete expressions (especially in South Africa itself) of genuine resistance to the fate that a failed liberation has imposed upon the region. These are the initial signs of what I have once hailed, in a particularly hopeful mood, as "the next liberation struggle"[3] and, while the manifestations of renewed resistance still remain, by and large, fledgling ones, they are, at the very least, harbingers of fresh hope.

* * *

In personal terms my own commitment to the liberation struggle in South Africa has been a long-standing one.[4] Thus my first extended sojourn in Africa was in Tanzania (reflected upon in chapter 2, below), a country on the very front lines of the struggle further south. There, where I taught for the best part of a decade in the 1960s and 1970s, I was privileged to

---

3   See my *The Next Liberation Struggle*, (*op. cit.*).

4   See, on this, my *Revolutionary Traveller* (*op. cit.*).

know, in the capital (Dar es Salaam), many of those directly engaged in the struggle further south – for Tanzania was then the vibrant staging ground for all the major movements of southern African exiles dedicated to liberating their own countries. This was particularly the case for Mozambique whose liberators first took me under their wing, as it were, and encouraged me to become actively involved in and supportive of their activities. And this in turn spilled over not only into contact with other of the region's liberation movements but also into deep involvement in the various solidarity networks, pegged to the support of struggles in Mozambique and in the other countries of southern Africa, that sprang up in Canada and in other parts of the western capitalist world.[5]

It bears noting that for many of us engaged in this regional struggle – whether we were denizens of the Global North or, more dangerously, of southern Africa itself – our engagement certainly nurtured a sense that victory against the region's diverse colonial and settler-driven racial tyrannies could be won. Not only that, however, we also sensed that such a victory might have – had even begun to have – profoundly radical and genuinely liberatory import for the vast masses of the impoverished of southern Africa, a liberation that could stretch beyond the promise of national independence and of the rights of ostensibly free citizens, important though such achievements undoubtedly might be. Sadly, we soon saw that things would prove to be not quite so straightforward. For no radical expansion of the meaning and import of "liberation" came readily to occur in the region, despite some real measure of "success" in each of the contested territories in southern Africa (see chapter 1 below). For such success only delivered, as I have described it in a previous volume, a liberation that was, in far too many ways, very "lite" indeed.[6]

---

5   See also, on this subject, my *A Partial Victory: The North American Campaign for Southern African Liberation in Global Perspective* (New York: Monthly Review Press, forthcoming).

6   See *Liberation Lite* (*op. cit.*).

In fact, such apparently anti-climactic outcomes were merely rationalized by the new regional elites, self-satisfied if also triumphant, as "inevitable" and "commonsensical" – blandly accepted with a kind of "globalization made me do it" air rather than being resisted in any meaningful way. As a result, both the word "liberation" and the struggle for it have come to have an increasingly impoverished import (see, again, chapter 1 below but also, for the Mozambican example of this outcome, chapter 3) – its meaning so narrowed as to now embrace only the goals of achieved racial and national assertion without, as already noted, any more expansive linkage being made to a challenging of extreme and persisting class and gender inequalities and without the realization of an effective empowerment of people through the full release of their democratic voice and energies.[7] Under such circumstances, to now sustain a commitment to a more expansive liberation in the region and further to hone the effort to realize it on the troubled ground of the present, has become an extremely challenging task. But, as we will also suggest, it is a far from insurmountable one.

* * *

Faced with such realities, some rethinking – as evidenced throughout this volume – of my overall perspective became increasingly imperative. In the first place it was necessary to adjust intellectually to the reality of the new "globalization" that has worked in recent decades to supplant the previous saliency of "conventional," more western and nationally-rooted, imperialisms and colonialisms, those which had sparked, in resistance to them, independence movements throughout the continent. Of course, resistance within the global South itself had already demonstrated a weakening of such specifically western-European imperialisms. But so too had the rise of a novel and over-arching super-imperialism, that of

---

7   John S. Saul, "Race, class, gender and voice: four terrains of liberation" (*ibid.*) and also John S. Saul, "The strange death of liberated southern Africa" (in Saul, *Decolonization and Empire, op. cit.*).

the United States, the key agent of a novel brand of neo-colonialism. And yet the new complexities within the camp of international capital did not stop there. Enter, stage right, "globalization" – what was this all about?

Clearly, "globalization" was both a concept and a reality, one that would have to be closely scrutinized…and, equally carefully, demystified. It did, for starters, refer to all the ways in which the world has become, to put it simply, smaller in recent decades – through, for example, the most dramatic of technological changes, from Skype to the Blackberry and so on. At the same time, and equally fundamental, was the fact that the evocative use of the word itself tended merely to blur the overbearing nature of the novel global economic relations it epitomized – and of the novel global political relations that were attendant upon them. What, to a crucially important degree, we now had in place of the nationally-premissed, western-sited, "Empires" that Africa had come to know all too well was indeed something new. For it was, first and foremost, an "Empire of Capital" itself, one that, through increasingly mobile capitalist enterprises, through supranational agencies (like the World Bank and the IMF) and through various intermediaries (the state elites of both capitalist countries at the "centre" of the system and those in command of most state apparatuses elsewhere [such as in South Africa]), now works actively to enforce the demands of global capital for profit and also to guarantee the (relative) stability of the overall system. As for Africa, what we now saw, under this novel imperial regimen, was a recolonization of the continent.

Note carefully what this formulation suggests. For, to repeat, this is a very different Empire from that produced by the European imperialisms/colonialisms that preceded it. And yet, at the same time, the ambiguous outcome of the freedom struggle – the region's "false decolonization" – in southern Africa very quickly came closely to resemble that which had characterized the more northern territories of Africa – and which, as we will remind ourselves in this book's conclusion (chapter 6), had been relentlessly critiqued by Frantz Fanon a half-century earlier. Then as now there was a crippling narrowing of an aspiration that had first seen liberation as heralding advance on the fronts of race, class and gender equality and in the assertion of democratic voice from below, with these seen as necessary complements to any racial and national demands. And it was precisely this reality that Fanon was critiquing in the 1950s and 1960s – as he would presumably do again today with reference to the countries of southern Africa were he still alive to witness their fate. In sum, spoils for the global centres and for their local intermediaries. For the rest: a singularly limited decolonization indeed.

Please permit me to reiterate here one central point made above, however: in making such a Fanonist assertion with reference to southern Africa there is absolutely no need to trivialize the importance of the region's defeat of racist colonialism and of apartheid, these victories representing a distinct advance in the ensuring of a genuine measure of racial equality. Yet one is also forced, I'm afraid, to again utter that "r" word: "recolonization" – substituting it for Fanon's word "neo-colonialism" as being more accurately descriptive for our own time. For this latter form of imperialism is being enacted by capital itself rather than primarily – as in the past – by some specific national (western) centre of empire or another.

As stated, we will return to Fanon's concerns in more detail in the concluding chapter of this book. Meanwhile, recall as well his observation that the new African elites or "middle-class," the "beneficiaries" of "neo-colonialism," who came to wield local power did so in a manner virtually unchecked domestically and to little or no positive and transformative effect as regards any genuine social and economic national advance on the part of the bulk of the populations concerned. The elites (principally, for Fanon, state-based elites) merely brandished the single party state and effective class dictatorship (even when there was more than one party) to supervise the pacification of the people, feeding the latter a diet of ethnic division and cruel overlordship – rather than encouraging them to have any on-going sense of their own possible empowerment. In fact, Fanon's litany of the "pitfalls" evidenced by post-colonial African history was formidable and grounded on a grim interrogation of the neo-colonial aftermath of African decolonization and independence that has been virtually unmatched by any analyst since.

And, to repeat, such a point of reference is still the one that remains most instructive for understanding southern Africa. True, as noted, the Empire of Capital is, in many of its implications for the global South, also different from the days when its more nationally-defined and restrictive predecessors were alone in imperialism's driver's seat. As suggested below, there is, within this new overall imperial system, (i) some greater room for (some) local states to manoeuvre on behalf of their own domestic ruling classes' interests in what is, for aspirant capitalists at least, a more truly competitive (if also more contradiction-ridden) global capitalist world; (ii) some greater room for national bourgeois classes in various settings to find some "national capitalist"/entrepreneurial space wherein to grow and to prosper; and (iii) even some greater room for certain states, working in conjunction with the capital (both foreign and domestic) lodged within their jurisdictions, to guide certain "sub-imperialisms" of their own devising.[8] For the fact is that capitalist actors are now much less restricted, in principle, in their actions by merely nationally-based centres of imperialistic capitalist activity than in the days of formal colonialism – although some such states (e.g., the United States with its military muscle) are still, self-evidently, powerful enough economically and politically to have pertinent and extremely damaging "imperial effects" in their own right.[9]

---

8   This latter role is, for example, one that South Africa has come to play vis-à-vis its neighbours in southern Africa. See, on this, D. Miller, O. Oloyede, R. Saunders (eds.), *South Africa in Africa – African Perceptions, African Realities*, a special issue of the *African Sociological Review*, 12, 1 (2008).

9   The extent to which the US itself can suffer due to the negative effects of the prioritizing – even by its "own" capital (acting as a key element of "global capital") – of a global logic of profit, rather than the implications for national economic well-being, is also much commented upon in recent literature. See, for example, Nayan

It is, in fact, the case that any overall imperial "logic" is now a much more volatile and unpredictable one than previously – as the trajectories of capitalisms ("successful" if also formidably unequal in their internal social implications) in, say, China, Korea and even India have demonstrated in recent decades. Yet what of southern/South Africa in this turbulent (and formidably unequal) world of twenty-first century capitalist imperialism? Truth to tell, given the extreme nature of its dependency and its still deeply subordinate economic position within the overall global system, the African setting provides much less prospect for even the distorted "benefits" of a capitalist "revolution" than do some other parts of the Global South.

As we shall see this is not an understanding that some aggressive southern African capitalists – like Armondo Guebuza, the current president of Mozambique (see chapter 3) or Moeletsi Mbeki (see chapter 6: "Conclusions") – would share. Nonetheless, the fact remains that if the immediate future of southern Africa is to be capitalist it will be, all signs indicate, primarily a capitalism driven by global interests and by capital's systemic priorities, one that fosters in Africa the extremely limited brand of development that may offer some wealth and power to the fortunate local few but does not do so to the vast majority of the impoverished population. And while the shifts in the broad pattern of world-wide capitalism will continue to require our critical examination for signs of change, it seems clear that, for the foreseeable future, recolonization as above defined and described seems set to remain the operative reality of both the region and the continent.

There is more bad news too. For southern Africa/South Africa also presents a situation in which the willed demobilization of their populations – away, that is, from any active transformative purpose – is the characteristic stance of the national leaderships. Certainly there are very few signs of the kind of innovative cultural rearmament of such

---

Chanda, "US Sours on Globalization: Protests may have abated, but globalization has fewer supporters in the US as job numbers don't add up," *Businessworld*, 25 May 2011 (online at Yale Center for the Study of Globalization).

populations that Fanon had glimpsed as possible after the transition from colonialism if leaderships were to take popular empowerment and genuinely principled practice seriously. Instead twenty and more years after "liberation" we see far too little evidence of the spark that "freedom" seemed to promise. To take merely one example, consider the gender-equality front of struggle in South Africa itself. For this latter was a focus of considerable radical energy during the country's transition period.

How sobering, then, it is to read over my morning's cup of coffee in one of this week's copies of Toronto's *Globe and Mail* the story by the paper's admirable South African correspondent, Geoffrey York. York is writing of the murder charge just laid against Olympian Oscar Pistorius, accused of murdering his female companion. But in the course of his account he (York) is forced to contextualize the event and to do so by recording that South Africa, more generally, is "a country with rising concerns about proliferating guns and rampant violence against women." In fact, he writes, "nearly 2,500 adult women have been murdered annually since 2007, one in four women has been raped and a woman is killed by an intimate partner every eight hours, studies have showed."[10] These are, needless to say, extremely alarming statistics.

To be sure, a day or two later, York can step back from some of the implications of such a story, arguing that "crime rates are falling, cities are being revitalized, streets are safer than they have been for 20 years, and the number of 'no go' areas is fast declining."[11] Well, maybe. At the same time it must also be admitted that, as in the case of gender concerns, alarming statistics and substantive anecdotal evidence – indices of the ANC's failure to fundamentally transform South African society – can still be cited in far too many areas of southern African life. This is true not only in the sphere of socio-economic betterment for the mass of South Africa's

---

10   Geoffrey York, "A nation fed up with 'femicide' shuns Pistorius," *The Globe and Mail* (February 18, 2013).

11   Geoffrey York, "The South Africa Being Described After The Shooting Of Reeva Steenkamp Is Not The Country I Know," *The Globe and Mail* (February 20, 2013).

population, of course. For the fact remains the population has not, by and large, been encouraged by the ANC to take real and effective ownership of their own lives and to join a process of collective empowerment and social advance.[12] In sum, South Africa has become, thus belying the promise of its liberation, merely an "ordinary country" as Neville Alexander once so tellingly termed it to be[13] – and not a particularly inspiring one at that.

***

Failures, then...but this is not the whole story, and this for reasons, I would argue, that go beyond the realities that York sees fit to allude to as he seeks to turn a fresh face to his story. For what of "resistance?" Is some further "rethinking" and re-tuning of emphases possible, even necessary, here? This, too, we will discuss in chapter 6. Nonetheless, it is certainly the case that both the recent history of struggle and the current reality of societies deeply divided along the lines of differential class, gender and political power seem to provide the perfect context for renewing the region's effort to win genuine freedom. True, this hasn't happened yet – as the smug and notoriously self-indulgent continuation in power of each of the founding liberation movements in the five countries of southern African "liberation" attests. Indeed, such movements-now-parties have been perfectly ready to reaffirm their hegemony, when necessary, at gunpoint – this being especially the case in Zimbabwe where Robert Mugabe has hung on to power through a series of stolen elections and against the expressed wishes (as registered at the voting-box) of a clear majority of his country's citizenry.

However, it is equally the case that, across the region, there is also a ticking time-bomb of frustration with the tangible failure of all previous liberation struggles. In consequence, a second southern African libera-

---

12   See below, but also, for more detailed analyses of this reality, the apposite chapters in Saul and Bond, *South Africa – The Present as History* (*op. cit.*).

13   Neville Alexander, *An Ordinary Country: Issues in the Transition from Apartheid to Democracy in South Africa* (Pietermaritzburg: University of Natal Press, 2002).

tion struggle seems to be entirely possible in the future – and not least in South Africa where, in particular, one can already see signs of the stirring of potentially effective and presumptively counter-hegemonic activity. We will have to say something more of this below (in chapter 4 on South Africa and, especially, in chapter 6 which contains this book's "Conclusions"). Nonetheless, in order to see this clearly we will also have to continue the work of clearing our minds of much that has blocked the deeper understanding of many on the left as to just what the reality of the current situation is. Indeed, as we will see, it is necessary to rethink quite fundamentally the terms of meaningful resistance and to identify more clearly than we have done the full range of attributes and preoccupations that mark those people who are most likely to contribute to any novel struggle.

I thus intend in this book to invoke some broader sense of the diverse components of genuine liberation, an intention that marks each of the essays included here. Thus, even in class terms, the struggle continues on more fronts than resort to a simple pseudo-leftist reductionism (to some all too familiar brand of "proletarian messianism" for example) might suggest. In chapter 5, for example, I seek to expand the language of the left beyond any such fetishism, a fetishism that, I fear, constrains our imaginations. This is not to substitute some kind of romantic "revolutionary nationalism" for the essentials of genuine class struggle (as some have charged) but rather to look to revolution as being informed by resistance to global capitalism certainly, but also to gender oppression, racist hegemony, non-democratic disempowerment, and environmental despoliation. And to imagine movements built as working coalitions of all those who resist inequality and oppression on each of these fronts. We on the left need make no apologies for such a politics.[14]

---

14   What of this kind of criticism of my straying from the path of true proletarian internationalism? Note, first, that nationalism has often been a key ingredient of liberation politics. For unequal national fates have long been a key aspect of the imperial reality and a certain nationalist concern can accurately focus some radical

In this respect, as I have noted elsewhere, South Africa's oppositional Democratic Left Front/DLF[15] carefully and quite self-consciously evokes, in its founding documents, a more expansive (and more accurate) notion of radical agency: specifically, the agency of both "the working-class and the poor." It is in chapter 5, cited above, that I advocate, to much the same purpose, the use of the terms "proletariat" and "precariat" to help parse much the same reality. But this is not all. As I have done in other of my recent writings and have restated here, I also emphasize the way in which a further range of related inequalities and oppressions can (and must) be linked to any effort on the part of "the working class and the poor" to realize progressive and socialist outcomes: such struggles, focussed on issues of racial and gender oppression, environmental concerns and the denial of people's expression of their genuine democratic voice, join class emancipation as essential features of the blue-prints for meaningful social, economic and political change.

In sum, the basis – however tentative, fragile and "in formation" this still may be – for a more meaningful regional "liberation" struggle exists (not least, in South Africa, the country of my own most sustained focus of

---

questioning of the global system and its logic – although international solidarity and common global struggle, as manifested in such initiatives as the World Social Forum process, may now seem even more promising. Nonetheless, expressions of nationalism can have a variety of quite diverse meanings and implications, depending on their actual context and content. What then can it mean to merely add, as some do, the somewhat sarcastic (in context) adjective "revolutionary" to "nationalism" to frame the phrase negatively for its dismissive use by many such critics? For the word "revolutionary," revolutionary in terms of resistance to global capitalism certainly, but also to gender oppression, racist hegemony, non-democratic disempowerment, and environmental despoliation is key. Of course, so defined, to be "revolutionary" demands recognition of the need for a far wider range of components to any coalition of relevant forces that aims to build a decent, comprehensive and truly liberatory socialism, on both national and global terrains, than many conventional leftist formulae permit. This adjective is thus crucial both to our understanding and to our action.

15   *Caveat lector*: This is an organization with which I myself have some modest affiliation.

attention in recent years). Indeed, one could even, in the last half of 2012, begin to sense the chance of realizing the necessary counter-hegemonic challenge that the imperatives of the time and the bleakness of the current situation there would seem to demand. In fact, the end of 2012 did indeed bring us some special hope for the prospect of a newly revolutionary South Africa. Interestingly 2012 was a year in which the country itself neared the twentieth anniversary of its victory over apartheid. And it was also a year that has signalled the celebration by the now-ruling ANC of the 100th anniversary of its own founding in 1912. Most importantly, however, it was also the year that witnessed the Marikana Massacre.

Marikana? The massacre there saw the gunning down by functionaries of the state's security apparatus of dozens of mineworkers engaged in industrial action against their employers and it revealed all too clearly just how bleak has become "the future" – as charted by the ANC since the overthrow of apartheid – that faces the vast majority of South Africans. Moreover, some South Africans have begun to speak and act out against that future, as the "Conclusion" to this book attests – drawing as it does on, inter alia, such findings as those of Peter Alexander (with his colleagues) and of others, regarding the recent wave of widespread unrest in South Africa's townships.[16] Of course, the present book is one that seeks primarily to provide a frame within which to view the current and future developments in the country and the region, and not to scan in any detailed way the auguries of the future itself.[17] But note the growing number of South

---

16 See Peter Alexander, Thapelo Lekgowa, Botsang Mmope, Luke Sinwell and Bongani Xezwi, *Marikana: A View from the Mountain and a Case to Answer* (Johannesburg, Jakana, 2012), but also Marcelle C. Dawson and Like Sinwell (eds.), *Contesting Transformation: Popular Resistance in Twenty-First Century South Africa* (London: Pluto Press, 2012), Peter Dwyer and Leo Zeilig, *African Struggles Today: Social Movements Since Independence* (Chicago: Haymarket Books, 2012) and Maria van Driel (ed.), *Remember Marikana* (Johannesburg: Khanya Publishing, 2012).

17 This book thus spells out rather less about Marikana and its aftermath than might a more journalistic and/or self-consciously up-to-the-minute volume. The reader is therefore invited to also consult the author's related attempt (with that of Patrick Bond) to assess in more detail both the meaning and the implications of "Mari-

Africans who now are beginning to speak out about their present doubts, as reflected, for example, in such reports as Mark Harris, "43% of SAns think country moving in wrong direction," one result of the recent Ipsos "Pulse of the People" poll released on February 13, 2013.

In fact, it is impossible not to hear in the sound and fury of Marikana the echoes of such notable earlier massacres in South Africa as those at Sharpeville and Soweto, massacres that similarly underscored the hollowness of the regime's – then the apartheid regime of course – claim for a rightful say as to South Africa's future. Moreover, such events, then and now, also spur further resistance to those in power. My conclusion, then, reflects both on the present moment and its disconcerting parallels to such earlier moments. But it seeks primarily merely to echo the voice of those South Africans who are already intimating alternative futures for their country: for them certainly, as well as for an ever increasing number of South/Southern Africans, the struggle must surely continue.

* * *

Forward, then, to the reading of this book. Let me merely close this introduction by thanking those comrades who, in both Africa and Canada, have made its writing possible. Notable, in the first instance, have been those I first knew in Mozambique's Frelimo in the '60s and '70s and also those in Canada's Toronto Committee for the Liberation of Southern Africa (TCLSAC). In particular, many of the latter group – the TCLSACers – have remained vital points of reference for me right up to the present. But so too have the many other southern Africans whom I have come to know while teaching, agitating and researching in their countries off and on over five decades. And there are other friends: like Roger Murray, Colin Leys, Jonathan Barker, the group around the Socialist Register, the

kana" – its overall context past and present, its specificity, its immediate aftermath and its longer-term implications – in chapters 6 and 7 of our closely related volume currently in press, Saul and Bond, *op. cit.,* as well as several of the sources cited in the previous footnote.

InfoServ crowd (notably Jim Kirkwood), those at Toronto's York University (students, teachers and staffers alike)...and, of course, my extended family.

Plus: my gratitude, once again, to my publisher Asad Zaidi in Delhi and, in the North Atlantic region, to the London-based Pluto Press (and especially to David Shulman there) and to Between the Lines in Toronto (and especially to Amanda Crocker), all of whom have shared in the actual realization of my manuscript as, finally, this book.

As for its dedication, it is to my friend Ruth First. For this book appears some thirty years since the day of her assassination at the hands of the apartheid state, an event that occurred just down the hall from my own office of the time at the University of Eduardo Mondlane in Mozambique; in fact, an appendix here is my recent presentation at a memorial symposium in her honour held at London's Institute of Commonwealth Studies where a project is also in train to digitize and preserve Ruth's papers. The latter will provide further intellectual nutriment, while evoking a rich example of commitment to those young scholars who now stand to learn – as I myself have done over the years – so much from a comrade like Ruth.

CHAPTER 1

The Failure of Southern African Liberation?[1]

Many of us came to southern Africa from the starting point of support for the peoples there who were struggling, in the 1960s, 1970s and 1980s, against the white minority/colonial regimes that dominated them and shaped so negatively their life chances. And, in this respect, there was of course to be a record of enormous achievement, one realised against great odds and especially so when that achievement is measured against the stunted expectations that many around the world had when the 30-year war for southern African liberation first announced itself in the early 1960s. Victory in southern Africa? Here, surely, was a dramatic African achievement to celebrate.

---

1   This essay first appeared as my editorial introduction to a series of articles on and about the fate of southern Africa in the wake of its ostensible liberation. This was first published as an e-issue of *AfricaFiles* – and here I must again acknowledge the assistance of Jim Kirkwood, Craig Hincks and Craig Dowler of the AfricaFiles Collective in Toronto for the crucial roles they played in preparing that earlier version of that symposium. The Africafiles symposium – which featured Henning Melber ("Namibia: a trust betrayed – again?"), David Sogge ("Angola: reinventing pasts and futures"), myself on Mozambique (see chapter 3 in this volume), Richard Saunders ("Zimbabwe: liberation nationalism – old and born-again"), and Patrick Bond ("South African splinters: from 'elite transition' to 'small-a alliances'") – also became, in somewhat revised form and with the same titles, a special themed section in the *Review of African Political Economy/ROAPE*, 36, #127 (March, 2011).

Well, yes and no. In fact, many in the worldwide liberation support/
anti-apartheid movement, seduced perhaps by the bold promises of the
liberation movements themselves, had come to understand that defining liberation merely in terms of national liberation from white colonial
dominance told, at best, half the story.[2] Important as it was to overcome
apartheid and similar racist structures in southern Africa, it was easy to
see that people in southern Africa were also seeking to liberate themselves
from class and corporate oppression, from structures of male domination,
and from authoritarian political practices. These goals came readily to
seem to be at least as important to any true liberation as was national
self-assertion. Nonetheless, the fact is that these attendant goals were to
fall by the wayside; indeed now, some decades after the fall of the most
visible forms of colonial and racial domination, it has become ever more
apparent just how narrow the definition of "liberation" has been permitted to become.[3]

For liberation in any expansive sense is, quite simply, something that
has not occurred in southern Africa. How to explain this? There has been,
for example, the global fall of socialism (at least in its Soviet form) and the
consequent loss of that particular point of reference and support. There
is, as well, the extreme nature of "historical backwardness" (in terms of
shortfalls in economic capacity and in the scarcity of requisite kinds of
expertise amongst the hitherto subject populations) that was bequeathed
as the legacy of the region's various ruthless colonialisms. And there has
been the vulnerability of the new indigenous elites (not least from the
ranks of the liberation movements themselves) to a too-easy seduction
into the ranks of privilege and self-interested power. And this in spite of
the fact that, in the period of the initial struggle for liberation, the ostensible aims of liberation movements were defined in terms of much more

---

2   See John S. Saul, "The strange death of liberated southern Africa" (*op. cit.*), and
     Saul, *Liberation Lite* (*op. cit.*).

3   Saul, "Race, class, gender and voice" (*op. cit.*).

transformative, even socialist, ends. In contrast to such "promises," the prevalence of starkly neo-colonial outcomes has been sobering.

Or think of it instead as having been a recolonization, one imposed by a new "Empire of Capital." Such a conceptualization arises from the fact that it is now much less easy than it was previously to disaggregate global capital into national capitals and to see any specific capital as being primarily attendant upon some nationally based imperialism and its colonialism. No, coming from the Global North and West (as it has done historically) but also now from the East (Japan, China and India), this new empire of linked capitals (competitive but interactive and fused together in novel ways as part of a global network of economic power) is what is currently recolonising Africa.[4] As suggested above, in our "Introduction" to this volume, nation-states (of both the North and the East) do still have an independent role with diverse raisons d'état that also play into the imperial equation. Nonetheless the globalization of capital has introduced something new to the workings of imperialism – principally a "colonization" of a novel type by a new empire (of capital), a recolonization of much of the global South in fact. True, such recolonization has been accomplished with the overt connivance of indigenous leaders/ elites – those who have inherited power with the demise of "white rule" but who, in doing so, have also manifested a far greater commitment to the interests of their own privileged class-in-creation than to those of the mass of their own people. But this merely reinforces the fact that this brave new world is far from being a happy one for the vast mass of southern African citizens – despite the freedom that they had seemed to have won.

A victory of sorts then. And now in the century's second decade we have already marked several key anniversaries. Take 2010 itself, the dawn of the decade in which this book has been written. This was a date that fell precisely fifty years after the launching, in 1960, of the "thirty years

---

4   On the "Empire of Capital," the "strange death of liberated southern Africa" and other related themes, see John S. Saul, *Decolonization and Empire* (*op. cit.*).

war (1960–1990) for southern African liberation," 35 years after the year of Angola's and Mozambique's independence, more or less 30 years after the day of independence in Zimbabwe, and a full 20 years after both Namibia's inaugural day and the release from prison of Nelson Mandela that marked so clearly the first of the very last days of apartheid (days of transition that would culminate in Mandela's election as president in 1994). There has been something to celebrate then, yet it is a sad fact that one already felt in 2010, and even more forcefully by mid-decade, compelled to ask the question as to just who actually won the struggle for southern African liberation. As I continued, having elsewhere framed precisely this question:

> We know who lost, of course: the white minorities in positions of formal political power (whether colonially in the Portuguese colonies or quasi-independently in South Africa and perhaps in Rhodesia/Zimbabwe). And thank fortune, and hard and brave work, for that. But who, in contrast, has won, at least for the time being: global capitalism, the West and the IFIs [international financial institutions], and local elites of state and private sectors, both white and black. But how about the mass of southern African populations, both urban and rural and largely black? Not so obviously the winners, I would suggest, and certainly not in any very expansive sense. Has it not been a kind of defeat for them too?[5]

How much of a defeat? Various country case studies – like those that comprised the body the Africafiles/Roape symposium that this chapter first served to introduce – did, cumulatively, give a very clear sense of the reality of this defeat.[6] Merely note here that in South Africa, for example, the economic gap between black and white has indeed narrowed statistically – framed by the fact that some blacks have indeed got very much richer (from their own upward mobility as junior partners to recolonization and from the fresh spoils of victory that this has offered

---

5   See John S. Saul, "Liberation support and anti-apartheid work as seeds of global consciousness: the birth of solidarity with Southern African struggle" in Karen Dubinsky, et al., eds. *New World Coming: the Sixties and the Shaping of Global Consciousness* (Toronto: Between the Lines, 2009), 139–140 and also Saul, *Revolutionary Traveler* (*op. cit.*).

6   As cited in footnote 1, above.

them). Yet the gap between rich and poor is actually wider than it ever was – and it is growing.

Much valuable research (by the likes of Terreblanche, McDonald, and Nattrass and Seekings[7]) documents this harsh fact – and other similarly sobering facts – and its stark implications. But note also the intervention several months ago by a leading South African prelate, Rev. Fuleni Mzukisi, who charged that poverty in South Africa is now worse than apartheid and is, in fact, "a terrible disease." As he said: "Apartheid was a deep crime against humanity. It left people with deep scars, but I can assure you that poverty is worse than that . . . People do not eat human rights; they want food on the table."[8]

This outcome is the result, most generally, of the grim overall inequalities between the global North and the global South that, as in many other regions, mark southern Africa. But, more specifically, it also reflects the choice of economic strategies in this latter region that can now imagine only elite enrichment and the presumed "trickle down benefits" of unchecked capitalism as being the way in which the lot of the poorest of the poor might be improved there. How far a cry this is from the populist, even socialist, hopes for more effective and egalitarian outcomes that originally seemed to define the development dreams of all the liberation movements. Indeed, what is especially disconcerting about the present recolonization of the region under the flag of capitalism is that it has been driven by precisely the same movements (at least in name) that led their countries to independence in the long years of overt regional struggle. But

---

7   See Sampie Terreblanche, *A History of Inequality in South Africa, 1652–2002* (Scottsville: University of Natal Press, 2002), Michael McDonald, *Why Race Matters in South Africa* (Cambridge and London: Harvard University Press, 2006), and Nicoli Nattrass and Jeremy Seekings, *Race, Class and Inequality in South Africa* (New Haven and London: Yale University Press, 2005).

8   Fuleni Mzukisi, as cited in Fredrick Nzwili, "South Africa: Pastor Says Poverty is Worse than Apartheid," from *Ecumenical News International*, circulated by AfricaFiles (10 September 2008).

just why this should have occurred, how inevitable it was, is something that demands careful consideration.

To be sure, the record varies somewhat from country to country. Thus, Mozambique under Frelimo (a case-study of which is included as chapter 3 in this volume), once the most forthrightly socialist of all the region's countries, has had to abandon that claim. True, it has also abandoned its initial brand of developmental dictatorship in favour of a formal democratization that has stabilised the country – albeit without markedly empowering the mass of its people or improving their socio-economic lot. Indeed, a recent textbook by Bauer and Taylor on southern Africa (a book of sympathetic though not notably radical predisposition) notes that the election to the presidency of Armando Guebuza who is the "holder of an expansive business empire and one of the richest men in Mozambique hardly signals that Frelimo will attempt to run anything but a globalist, neo-liberal agenda – regardless of the abject poverty suffered by most of the electorate."[9]

As for Angola it has, until quite recently, experienced a much greater and more dramatic degree of divisive fragmentation than Mozambique – although its antidote to that, since the death of Jonas Savimbi, has had as little to do with popular empowerment and broad-based development as have the present policies of its fellow ex-Portuguese colony, Mozambique. In fact, it has been argued that it is only a handful of progressive international initiatives (Human Rights Watch, Global Witness and the like) that have had some success in holding the feet of exploitative corporations and of Angola's own government to the fire of critical scrutiny. For unfortunately, as David Sogge argues in his essay on Angola in the original symposium (see footnote 1, above), the country's own population, battle-scarred and battle-weary, has been rather slower to find effective

9   Gretchen Bauer and Scott Taylor Bauer, *Politics in Southern Africa: state and society in transition* (Boulder, CO: Lynne Rienner, 2005), p. 135; also Joe Hanlon and Teresa Smart, *Do Bicycles Equal Development in Mozambique?* (London: Boydell and Brewer, 2008).

means to exert their own claims. Yet, as the same Bauer and Taylor volume quoted above feels forced to conclude of Angola, oil money and corruption have merely "exacerbated the already glaring discrepancies between rich and poor" and have, "quite simply, threatened the country's recovery and future development."[10]

Meanwhile Zimbabwe, in the brutal thrall of Mugabe and Zimbabwe African National Union (ZANU), has witnessed an even greater deterioration of national circumstances than either of these two countries. There, say Bauer and Taylor, "the ZANU-PF's stewardship of the economy [has] been an unmitigated disaster,"[11] while its politics, through years of overt and enormously costly dictatorial practices, have produced a situation, as Richard Saunders details (in his own essay in the original AfricafFiles/ Roape symposium that followed this essay/introduction[12]), that is proving enormously difficult both to displace and to move beyond.

The results in both Namibia[13] and South Africa, even if not quite so bloody as those produced by Renamo's war, the prolonged sparring of Savimbi with the Popular Movement for the Liberation of Angola (MPLA) and Mugabe's depredations, are not much more inspiring in terms of effective mass empowerment and broad-gauged human betterment – as the cited articles by Henning Melber and Patrick Bond demonstrate.[14] Thus, a long-time and firmly loyal African National Congress (ANC) cadre (Ben Turok) has himself, in a recent book entitled *The Evolution of ANC Economic Policy*, acknowledged both the contribution of ANC poli-

---

10 Bauer and Taylor, *ibid.*, p. 163.

11 Bauer and Taylor, *ibid.*, p. 197; also Brian Raftopoulos and A. Mlambo, *Becoming Zimbabwe: A History from the Pre-colonial Period to 2008* (Harare: Weaver Press, 2009).

12 Richard Saunders, "Zimbabwe: liberation nationalism – old and born-again," *ROAPE*, #127 (March, 2011).

13 Henning Melber, *Re-examining Liberation in Namibia: Political Culture since Independence* (Uppsala: Nordiska Afrikainstitutet, 2003).

14 See, again, footnote 1.

cies to growing inequality in his country while reaching "the irresistible conclusion that the ANC government has lost a great deal of its earlier focus on the fundamental transformation of the inherited social system"![15]

In sum, South Africa, like the other "liberated" locales of the region, has become, in the sober phrase with which Neville Alexander[16] has titled a book of his own on South Africa's transition from apartheid to democracy, merely "an ordinary country" – despite the rather finer future that many, both in southern Africa and beyond, had hoped would prove to be the outcome of the long years of liberation struggle. But Alexander's characterization could be said to apply to all of the countries in the region: what we now have, instead of a liberated southern Africa that is vibrant, humane and just, is a region of a very different sort indeed.

Moreover, not only is there deepening inequality within countries but, in the region taken as a whole, there is also – to take one glaring example – a situation in which South Africa's capitalist economic power now merely complements global capitalist power in holding the impoverished people of southern Africa in quasi-colonial thrall (as a recent series of articles in *Africa Files Ezine* on South Africa in the southern Africa region has recently documented[17]) – while doing disturbingly little to better the lot of such people, the vast majority both in South Africa and elsewhere. Or take the Southern African Development Community (SADC): it has become (albeit with a few honourable exceptions) primarily a club of presidents that reveals itself to be – as the sad case of its kid-gloves treat-

---

15   Ben Turok, *The Evolution of ANC Economic Policy: From the Freedom Charter to Polokwane* (Cape Town: New Agenda, 2008), p. 263.

16   Neville Alexander, *An Ordinary Country: Issues in the Transition from Apartheid to Democracy in South Africa* (Pietermaritzburg: University of Natal Press, 2002); see also William Gumede, *Thabo Mbeki and the Battle for the Soul of the ANC*. London: Palgrave MacMillan, 2008).

17   Richard Saunders (ed.), "South Africa in Africa," an AfricaFiles series of articles running monthly from May to September, 2008, (at http://www.africafiles.org/ atissueezine.asp?issue=issue8), this series then forming the core of D. Miller, O. Oloyede, R. Saunders (eds.), *South Africa in Africa* (*op. cit.*).

ment of Zimbabwe and its backing of an otherwise deservedly embattled Mugabe amply demonstrates – more a source of tacit support for the status quo than a force for facilitating any kind of just transition to effective democracy in Zimbabwe.

In truth, it is now often said by people of a Left persuasion that the current global situation offers no real alternatives, no real hope, for Africa (including southern Africa). It cannot, they say, count on any plausible socialist alternative.[18] Moreover, a seasoned observer like Giovanni Arrighi can only urge Africa to look to a relatively benign China (a doubtful haven of hope, one fears) and/or to the kinder and gentler practices of its own elites in order to realise even a marginal adjustment to its desperate plight.[19] Others fall back on the equally unlikely prospect of a revolution-ary transformation of the exploitative West to then lift many of the key barriers to a brighter future. Thus, as one friend has recently written to me: "I don't see how the South can ever liberate itself in the absence of a new socialist project becoming powerful in the North." Yet he feels forced to add that "I don't see that happening until people are hurting and see no prospect of meeting their personal needs under globalized neoliberalism, and until a new left movement with a serious attitude to organization and democracy." But this is a faint hope too, my correspondent – who confesses to feeling "very pessimistic" – obviously fears.

Failing a revolution in the global capitalist centres, however, what are the actual prospects for some dramatic change occurring within the region itself, one, necessarily, driven from below? The present author has called elsewhere for "a next liberation struggle"[20] in southern Africa for precisely this reason, a struggle, like the one that is currently afoot in

18   See, for example, Gabriel Kolko's deeply unsettling but also highly problematic *After Socialism: Reconstructing Critical Social Thought* (New York: Routledge, 2006).

19   Giovanni Arrighi, "The African crisis," *New Left Review*, 15 (May–June, 2002), pp. 5–36; for a critique of Arrighi's position see Saul, "Arrighi and Africa," *Review of African Political Economy*, 36 (122), 644–649 (2009).

20   John S. Saul, *The Next Liberation Struggle* (*op. cit.*).

several places in Latin America for example, that seeks to at least neutralise the intervention of imperialist forces from the North while also facilitating the empowerment of its own people in political and economic terms.

And there are localised and grassroots resistances in the region in a wide variety of settings and on a broad range of policy fronts that seek to make headway and even to begin to add up to potential hegemonic alternatives to the failed liberation movements that we still see in power. Moreover, some attempts to so resist – the initial rise of the Movement for Democratic Change (MDC) in opposition to Mugabe, for example, and the removal of the brazen Thabo Mbeki from South Africa's presidency before the end of his term; the dramatic grassroots resistance, especially in South Africa, to the AIDS pandemic that stalks the entire region; and the signs of a resurgent economic nationalism that threatens to renegotiate contracts with the private sector and even to reverse certain privatizations – do begin to so promise: promise, that is, to "add up," even if, to this point, "not quite" and certainly "not yet"!

So the question remains: how might one hope, even expect, that the diverse instances of resistance that are visible could come to pose hegemonic alternatives in southern Africa to the recolonization that has been the fate of that part of the continent in the wake of its seeming "liberation"? What might Africans on the ground in the region have to do next, and how can they best be supported from outside in doing so? Equally importantly, how might residents of the global North organise themselves in order – with respect to any "next liberation support struggle" – to best assist them: staying the hand of our own governments and corporations on the one hand, and speaking out clearly and effectively on behalf of such movements for genuine liberation on the ground, on the other? One thing is clear: the liberation struggle continues. We cannot live in the (recent) past. We must act to shape the future.

The liberation of southern Africa, then. And its aftermath. A story full of heroism, but also, in many ways, a grim tale, even if the right people – the arrogant white elites who once dominated, in racist terms, southern Africa – had lost. But, in the longer run, it is important to ask, who really won? Not, visibly and in any very expansive sense, the vast mass of the southern Africa people. Instead, the spoils of victory have mainly gone to "global capitalism" on the one hand, and to that thin stratum of black elites who have since arrogated to themselves whatever power and privilege global capital has left to them, on the other.

I am, of course, well aware that "the struggle continues" – although the forces who actively wage it may be still fragmented and relatively weak. Indeed, the extent to which most southern African governments, through SADC, have closed ranks behind the villainous Mugabe is a sobering index of the challenge that continues to confront the people of southern Africa. For, evidence from throughout the region clearly demonstrates, the realities of Zimbabwe are duplicated (albeit in somewhat less graphic terms) on each of the region's erstwhile fronts of liberation struggle.

Yet we know too that there are also seeds of resentment and of resistance throughout the region. Moreover, some of us remember quite vividly just how bleak the prospect for redress of racist rule in the region seemed in the 1960s. Nonetheless, the apartheid regime, and its cancerous ilk of racist hierarchies located throughout the sub-continent, fell. And now it is again just possible to catch a glimpse of often impressive stirrings of popular resistance that continue to disrupt the overweening pretensions of the temporary "winners." Perhaps it is too early to say that "vitoria é certa" – over and against such "winners" and as envisaged by such challengers to their present hegemony – but it is certainly not presumptuous to say, with reference to all the emergent bearers of a fresh liberation struggle, "a luta continua."

CHAPTER 2

Tanzania Fifty Years On (1961–2011)
Rethinking Ujamaa, Nyerere and Socialism in Africa[1]

December 8, 1961. A little over fifty years ago: Tanzanian Independence Day (it was actually still Tanganyika then, until the union with Zanzibar a few years later changed the country's name to Tanzania). But, of course, many countries in Africa were obtaining their independence from the British and French colonial states in those years. What set Tanzania apart in the 1960s, much as Ghana had been set apart, in the 1950s, by Kwame Nkrumah's "Black Star" (as Basil Davidson once entitled a book chronicling Osageyfo's moment of ascendancy) was Nyerere's own star. For the latter was then, and however briefly, on its ascent, with Nyerere linked, by the late 1960s, to the moment of "Ujamaa" – and to the possibility, even the promise, of a distinctive socialism in Africa that could be the touchstone for something beyond the kind of "neo-colonialism" and "false decolonization" that great thinkers like Frantz Fanon had already identified as the sobering stigmata of the overall African decolonization

---

1   On November 28, 2011 I presented a version of this essay, subsequently published in much the present form in *ROAPE*, #131 (March, 202), at an Oxford seminar. I also drew on a related paper that I had recently published in a special issue of the Tanzanian journal *Chemchemi* (Issa Shivji, et. al., *Chemchemi*, 4/5 [200]) prepared, quite specifically, "in celebration of 50 years of Tanzanian independence."

process. Time, perhaps, to revisit that Nyerere moment, that Ujamaa moment, and to evaluate it afresh.

Of course, one must pause at the outset at the very term "African socialism." Perhaps the most notable further attempt to construct a meaningful socialism in Africa came in the early "socialist" years of Mozambique's post-liberation emergence (which, as with the case of Tanzania, I had the opportunity of witnessing, off and on but at close hand, during much of its all too brief life-span and I also reflect upon that country in the following chapter). But the Mozambican leaders I knew were actually very scornful of the concept "African socialism" and indeed of Tanzania's own "socialist" practices (which didn't stop them from making many similar mistakes themselves, it should be emphasized.) They (as they affirmed forcefully) were socialists in Africa, not "African socialists."

Tanzanians are speaking for themselves on this subject, of course, as witness such recent books as Chambi Chachage and Annar Cassam's edited volume *Africa's Liberation: The Legacy of Nyerere*[2] and an illuminating special issue of the Dar es Salaam-based journal *Chemchemi*.[3] Indeed, I was myself honoured with an invitation to contribute to the latter *Chemchemi* symposium and it is from my essay there that I will principally draw many of the observations that appear in the present chapter, observations appropriate, I hope, to celebrate both the fiftieth anniversary of the independence moment that inspires them and the memory of the man, Nyerere, who personified that independence moment as well as the subsequent Ujamaa experiment itself.

I also have the privilege of recalling all of this at first hand, if not precisely of the moment of independence itself then of its immediate aftermath, the "ujamaa years." For I had the opportunity to live and work

---

2   Chachage, Chambi and Annar Cassam, eds., *Africa's Liberation: The Legacy of Nyerere* (Cape Town, Dakar, Nairobi and London: Pamabazuka Press, 2010).

3   Issa Shivji with Adolf Mkenda, Opportuna Kweka and Jacquiline Mgumia, eds. "Special Combined Issue" of *Chemchemi* (Dar es Salaam), 4 and 5, "in celebration of 50 years of Tanzanian independence" (2011).

in Dar es Salaam for seven exciting years in the 1960s and early 1970s, years which, to my good fortune, were, precisely, the years of the Arusha Declaration and of Ujamaa in their fullest flower.[4] Indeed, it is the emotions of that time as well as my sober reflections over some fifty years regarding things Tanzanian that I bring to this chapter.

* * *

The "moment" of Ujamaa may have been brief but in the late sixties and early seventies Tanzania was certainly an exciting place to be. True, as we will see, the implications of what had been begun with the Arusha Declaration in 1968 were just too dangerous and too radical even for its initial champion, Julius Nyerere. Thus, while Horace Campbell[5] is correct to eulogize Nyerere himself as "a great human being who demonstrated his respect for the ordinary African and for the lives of all human beings" (and Campbell then proceeds to compile a convincing list of Nyerere's many achievements), the continent will learn too little by not also registering the man's – and the ujamaa project's – weaknesses. As Firoz Manji explicitly notes in his own preface to *Africa's Liberation*: while we "should not be shy in celebrating his achievements…at the same time, he would be among the first to condemn any attempts to romanticise his period in office."[6] It is in this spirit that I offer the present chapter.

---

4   See Lionel Cliffe and John S. Saul, eds., *Socialism in Tanzania*, volume I, "*Politics*" and volume 2, "*Policies*" (Nairobi: East African Publishing House, 1972 and 1973) and Giovanni Arrighi and John S. Saul, *Essays on the Political Economy of Africa* (New York: Monthly Review Press, 1973), especially ch. 6.

5   Horace Campbell, "Julius Nyerere: between state-centred and people-centred Pan-Africanism" in Chachage and Cassam (*op. cit.*).

6   Firoze Manji, "Preface" to Chachage and Cassam, *op cit.*, p. xx. As Annar Cassam also adds in her "Introduction" to this same volume (p. xx): "The words 'living memory' acquire a deeper meaning when one considers the place that Mwalimu Julius Nyerere occupies in the minds, hearts, lives, consciousness and subconscious of those who knew him and those who did not, those who live in Tanzania and those who do not, those who pay attention to Africa and those who judge it, from near and afar."

Thus Nyerere spoke of empowering the people and, with *Mwongozo* – Tanganyika African National Union/TANU Guidelines 1971 – seemed to have persuaded his fellow TANU leaders actually to embrace the notion of genuine control, by the people, from below. Yet when that same "people" actually began to move – workers at the Mount Carmel Rubber Factory, peasants in Ruvuma, students at the university[7] – Nyerere joined with the state and its bureaucrats, political and administrative, to slash back: to crush the workers, to smash the Ruvuma Development Association (and then forward "Ujamaa Vijini" only from on high and by means of a self-defeating policy of "enforced villagization"), and to have student president Simon Akivaga whisked away from the campus and summarily dispatched back home to his native Kenya in a waiting plane: his crime, apparently, having been to invoke the *Mwongozo* directive, with its official encouragement of the exercise of power from below, in criticism of the university's hierarchy![8] Tanzania: an exciting place, momentarily, to be, then, but ultimately and in many ways a sad and defeated one.

Against my memories of the excitement of the time two images pull me back to sobriety. One was the aforementioned Akivaga incident, seared in my mind as the cold wind of reality and of a very different kind of memory blow through it. Here I refer to the invasion of the campus of

7   On the workers see, *inter alia*, Pascal Mihyo, "The Workers Revolution in Tanzania," *MajiMaji* (Dar es Salaam), #17, August, 1974 (this also appears, in edited form, in *The Review of African Political Economy/ROAPE*, 4: 62–84) and Henry Mapolu (ed.), *Workers and Management* (Dar es Salaam: Tanzania Publishing House, 1976); on the peasants in Ruvuma, Leander Schneider, "Developmentalism and its failings: why rural development went wrong in 1960s and 1970s Tanzania," Ph.D dissertation, Columbia University, 2003 and "Freedom and Unfreedom in Rural Development: The Theory and Practice of Julius Nyerere's Rural Socialism," in *Canadian Journal of African Studies*, 38, 2 (2004); and, on the students at the university, John S. Saul, *Revolutionary Traveller* (*op. cit.*), ch. 1, "The 1960s – Tanzania," and Michelle Borbonniere, "Debating Socialism on the Hill: The University of Dar es Salaam. 1961–71," M.A. dissertation, Dalhousie University, 2007.

8   Borbonniere (*ibid.*, p. 146) concludes that "The Akivaga crisis, which was seen as a failure to follow through on the promise of *Mwongozo* at the university, was the first [sic] indication of a gap between Nyerere's political theory and practice."

the University of Dar es Salaam by the Field Force Unit in 1970. Standing nearby, I saw my own student Akivaga, the Kenyan leader of the University Student Council who, having been summoned for a meeting with the principal, was then dragged, at gun-point, down the cement stairs at the front of the administration building, tossed like a sack of old clothes into a waiting army vehicle and sped away to his expulsion both from the university and from the country.

No more can I forget those (admittedly few) Tanzanian faculty members who had tended to side with the students at the time, for they were also to be disciplined (as were a number of us non-Tanzanians, who were very soon to find our contracts not renewed). Arnold Temu of the History Department provides a particularly sobering case in point: thrown out of Parliament for questioning the regime's handling of university matters and later sacked from the university itself, he was soon sent effectively into exile as an itinerant academic. Indeed, one of the most poignant moments of a research trip I took to Dar es Salaam in the summer of 2001 was my running into Arnold, our subsequent chat then bringing, unsolicited, a startling statement from him: he had sworn to himself not to return to live in Tanzania as long as Nyerere was alive. He thus offered a perspective on "Mwalimu" and his "democratic sensibility" that is, at the very least, worth pondering.[9]

Much else was happening, at least momentarily, of a far more positive nature, of course. After all, this was the period when Fanon was writing eloquently of the dangers of a neo-colonialism spearheaded by, precisely,

9   I draw here on my account of the Akivaga and Temu cases to be found in John S. Saul, "Julius Nyerere's Socialism: Learning from Tanzania," which is chapter 7 of my *The Next Liberation Struggle: Capitalism. Socialism and Democracy in Southern Africa* (Toronto, Durban, New York and London: Between the Lines, University of KwaZulu/Natal Press, Monthly Review Press and Merlin Press, 2005). Nor can I, as further evidence of the texture of the approach of the Tanzanian state under Nyerere both to "*Mwongozo*" and to "academic freedom," ignore the first-hand accounts of other witnesses who, a few years later (1978), recorded the way in which protesting students were savagely beaten by security forces as they marched in protest down the Morogoro Road to town.

the emergent African elite itself. And this potential problem was exactly what the Arusha Declaration and *Mwongozo* seemed, equally eloquently, to be about: a concrete attempt to control elitism within the ranks of the newly emergent nations. True, both declarations were more powerful in their mere statement than in the substance of their realization. Yet I have found some of the most forthright (and most Fanonist!) perspectives on the post-colonial reality to surface during the Arusha years – perhaps most strikingly in a newspaper account (in *The Nationalist*) of a public speech given by Nyerere at that time:

> Nyerere called on the people of Tanzania to have great confidence in themselves and to safeguard the nation's hard-won freedom. Mwalimu [Nyerere] warned that the people should not allow their freedom to be pawned as most of their leaders were purchasable. He warned further that in running the affairs of the nation the people should not look on their leaders as saints and prophets.

> The President stated that the attainment of freedom in many cases resulted merely in the change of colours, white faces to black faces without ending exploitation and injustices, and above all without the betterment of the life of the masses. He said that while struggling for freedom the objective was clear but it was another thing to remove your own people from the position of exploiters.[10]

This sounds good but was a lot more of substance actually possible? Much of the scholarly debate of the time centred on this question. Tanzania was, after all, a small, economically backward country, with, it was argued, no really strong and coherent internal class forces pressing from below. There were also global constraints of course: neo-colonial pressures and the like. Most strikingly, however, much of the country's radical project seemed to have been hatched in the sensibility of one man, a man (Nyerere) who had, as we know, his own limitations, both of possibility (vis-à-vis his own colleagues and vis-à-vis the external world), but also of vision. Of course, Nyerere did remain usefully suspicious of the congealing Western-dominated global system. Unfortunately, however, and despite his (entirely accurate) nervousness about the Soviet Union and

---

10   *The Nationalist* (Dar es Salaam), issue of September 5, 1967.

its own "alternative" model, he was not strengthened in his thinking by a reluctance to give any very clear Marxist resonance and analytical edge to his voice as a critic of imperialism and global capitalism.

True, he did continue to offer a usefully critical voice, remaining one of the sharpest commentators on the negative role of the International Financial Institutions/IFIs until the very end of his life. Moreover, he committed both himself and Tanzania to the on-going liberation of southern Africa – although here it was also unfortunate that he did not envisage any particularly democratic or expansively liberated future for the people of the countries of southern Africa so freed (as foreshadowed by Nyerere's taking the accused "leaders" of the South West Africa People's Organization/SWAPO opposition into Tanzania's own custody when the latter, seized by the Zambian army on behalf of Sam Nujoma and the SWAPO elite, threatened to seek their legal self-defense through the right to *habeas corpus* still available to them in Zambia – but not in Tanzania!).[11] Yet Nyerere did counsel staying the course of the struggle in the southern part of the continent and it is also true that with regard to Frelimo in Mozambique, for example, he backed, against the strident opposition of some of his own ministers, the most committed of the movement's leaders in the internal struggle that followed the assassination of Eduardo Mondlane.

These latter incidents were important, of course. For, whatever their other implications, Nyerere's lack of democratic sensibility with reference both to internal dynamics of the regional liberation struggle (in the SWAPO case if not the Mozambican one) as well as to Tanzania itself was troubling in more general terms. Thus, for all his own suspicion of the Soviet Union, Nyerere embraced, for Tanzania itself, an all too similar vanguard party model to that which the Soviets exemplified – even if he sought to sweeten that system with an ingenious (too ingenious?) innova-

---

11   Colin Leys and John S. Saul, "Liberation without democracy: The SWAPO crisis of 1976," *Journal of Southern African Studies*, 20, 1 (March, 1994), pp. 123–147.

tion of his own: "one-party democracy." In short, "Mwalimu" as "teacher" too often became, at best, the benign autocrat of the class-room and, at worst, a stern and officious head-master – at great long-run cost, one fears, to the emergence of a strong and self-confident citizenry. Indeed, if one had not learned to be sufficiently suspicious of the vanguard party model from the experience of socialism in Eastern Europe, Tanzania and Mozambique would have been useful refresher courses as to the real price to be paid for choosing uncritically what was, in essence if not always in name, a vanguardist option.

Neither TANU nor Frelimo quite learned enough about the complex dynamics of rural development either. For the suspicion of peasants – as of any genuinely democratic empowerment of the mass of the population from below – proved to run deep in Tanzania and the same, for all their criticisms of Tanzania's own practice, was equally true of the Mozambican leadership. Thus, in spite of their many statements as to the crucial "class belonging" (as workers and peasants!) of "the people," such class descriptors were all too readily collapsed into merely populist categories – instead of their facilitating a view of such "classes" as being potentially "empowerable" in genuinely radical terms.

As Leander Schneider (one of the most careful and incisive of all scholars of the "ujamaa vijini" initiative) suggests, in this central rural policy

> several of the most inspiring strands of Nyerere's politics flow together – in particular, an exemplary commitment to improving the condition of the poor, as well as his theorizing about the nexus of development, freedom, empowerment, and participation. However, it is also in the field of rural development that problematic dimensions of Nyerere's leadership become, perhaps, most starkly apparent. Not only did the policy of enforced ujamaa/villagization fail to improve the material conditions of Tanzania's rural population, but the adoption of coercive means to further it also points to the authoritarian side of Nyerere's rule.[12]

---

12   Schneider (*op. cit.*, 2004).

The word "authoritarian" is not chosen lightly by Schneider. In fact, its use lies at the very centre of the argument he wishes to make. Nor is it accidental that he concludes his analysis, of what he calls the "statist bent and the related overtly coercive character observed in the 1970s Tanzania," with the observation that "Tanzanian history shows, above all, that turning a blind eye to the tensions of participatory development will neither make them go away nor allow one to avoid the serious costs implied by swiftly reducing participation to near meaninglessness." Shocking then that much-cited analysts like Cranford Pratt can demur somewhat at Nyerere's *too leftist* economic policies but laud him for his fervent embrace of democracy! Because, put quite simply, the latter emphasis is almost entirely inaccurate.

In this connection I am forced to recall an all-too-acrimonious debate I had several decades ago with Pratt himself regarding the Tanzanian experience. Pratt professed to find in my then criticisms of Tanzania's politics a preference for an approach that was far more dangerously and self-righteously authoritarian, far too Marxist and Leninist, than anything that Nyerere was inclined towards. Indeed, for Pratt, Nyerere's political practice was essentially democratic, albeit a practice that sought assertively to guide from above the consolidation of democracy in such a way that the country could weather the very real threats to national consolidation that Pratt apparently thought to characterize the immediate post-independence years.

For my part, while rejecting Pratt's charge that I had favoured some extreme and overtly authoritarian approach (although I did later concede that I myself had erred in too uncritically sanctioning, especially in Mozambique, the embrace of "vanguardism"), I argued that Pratt had himself quite seriously underestimated both the authoritarian nature of Nyerere's own "democratic" practice and the very high costs that the president's chosen methods (and those of TANU, the party he led) had inflicted upon the movement for progressive change in Tanzania. Accepting, at the time and with Pratt, the prevailing framework of the one-party state, I argued that Nyerere's polity could only hope to provide this as a framework for nurturing democracy if popular forces – workers, peasants, students, women – were empowered to act quite dramatically from below in order to ensure the safeguarding of their own interests and the maintenance of a socialist direction for the country.[13] But this was not to be.

There are those who still argue at this point that Nyerere was merely blocked in his own high-minded intentions by the global realities of power and by recalcitrant politicians and bureaucrats in his own camp. There is some truth in this, of course, but not, I would argue, nearly enough to cover all the data nor to explain all the contradictions in the ujamaa project. Not that anyone would wish to argue that Nyerere's intentions were anything but "benign." Nor would one suggest that "Tanzanian socialism" could ever merely have sprung, "spontaneously," from the Tanzanian populace. No, *leadership*, clearly explaining costs and benefits and the complexities of seeking to realize progressive outcomes while helping to "raise popular consciousness," would inevitably have to have been part of any revolutionary political equation. And no doubt much of Nyerere's political practice squares with such a model. Yet surely twentieth century history has taught us, if nothing else, the extreme dangers of any such "leadership," even at its most benign, slipping the leash of popular control and doing what it perceives by its own lights to be "best" for its ostensibly "backward" wards. And just as surely one might legitimately fear that Nyerere drifted much too close to the authoritarian horn of this dilemma on numerous occasions for one to be entirely confident of his own good judgment in each case.

---

13   Here again – in writing on the views of both Pratt and Nyerere in these paragraphs – I draw on some of my own formulations in "Julius Nyerere's Socialism: Learning from Tanzania," which is chapter 7 of my *The Next Liberation Struggle: Capitalism. Socialism and Democracy in Southern Africa* (Toronto, Durban, New York and London: Between the Lines, University of KwaZulu/Natal Press, Monthly Review Press and Merlin Press, 2005), pp. 149–150 and 156 and where my perspective on such matters is advanced more extensively.

Additional support for Nyerere's political project is also offered by scholars precisely along the same lines originally hinted at by Pratt. Even if acknowledging (albeit somewhat *sotto voce*) that Nyerere may well have blunted the assertions of workers and peasants in Tanzania it is claimed that, in enacting a "guided democracy," he nonetheless derailed any too regionalist or "tribalist" political projects and this in the long-term interests of a unified and pacific Tanzania.[14] A tempting argument if one compares developments in Tanzania with those elsewhere on the continent. Yet one also recalls that it was often stated in the early days how fortunate Tanzania was both in the multiplicity of its diverse ethnicities (without any one being too overbearing numerically to be considered a particular threat by others) and in having Swahili as a national *lingua franca*. Some points may nonetheless be granted to TANU for its politics of self-consciously downgrading and transcending "tribalism" by means of "one-partyism" and the like, but, as noted, this was surely at the expense of any very radical form of "class struggle" – with the price of downplaying the latter being very high in terms of any prospective realization of a possible socialist outcome.

Moreover, any genuinely rural tilt in the country's macro-economic strategies was lost too. After all, economists like Samir Amin, in his own voluminous writings, have argued that only an ever more radical decolonization of Africa from central capitalist control – in Amin's dramatic word, in an actual "delinking" of the economies of the Global South from the Empire of Capital that otherwise holds the South in its sway – could actually be developmental in any meaningful sense.[15] Yet,

---

14   In this regard one notes the importance, shortly after independence, of the dramatic disempowering and rapid neutralization, by Nyerere and the new Tanganyikan state, of the various traditional authorities previously at work in Tanganiyika. This initiative is an important positive aspect of the Tanzanian story not well covered in the literature on the country to my knowledge (although I learned when in Oxford to present an earlier version of this essay, of a recent doctoral dissertation there by Festo Mkenda on this subject, which I have not yet read).

15   I have cited Amin's concept of "delinking" in preparing the essay "The Empire of

as Amin readily admits, there is no realistic haven of "autarky" that one can look to, no way of avoiding some involvement in the broader market (as opportunity, though not, he argues, as seduction). What must occur, however, is the substitution of the present political economy of recolonization with an alternative that tilts effectively towards "delinking" as a national goal – invoking an auto-centric socio-economic alternative that is at once effective, efficient and productive. What would the programme of a national strategy erected on the premise of a strong tilt towards radical delinking from the presently existent and profoundly cancerous global capitalist system look like? The answer to this question could only begin to be found in a new project of genuine socialist planning – established on a national or regional scale – that sought to smash, precisely, the crippling (il)logic of present "market limitations" upon development.

This, in turn, suggests the need for a programme that (following the formulations of Clive Thomas, the Guyanese economist who also taught in Tanzania) would embody "the progressive convergence of the demand structure of the community and the needs of the population"[16] – this being the very reverse of the market fundamentalist's global orthodoxy. One could then ground a "socialism of expanded reproduction" (in the name of the presumed imperatives of accumulation), one that refuses

---

Capital, Recolonization and Resistance: Rethinking the Political Economy of Development in the Global South" for its inclusion in my *Revolutionary Traveller* (*op. cit.*), pp. 354-367, and I have here only mildly recrafted that argument for present purposes. "Delinking" is defined, by Amin, as "the submission of external relations [to internal requirements], the opposite of the internal adjustment of the peripheries to the demands of the polarizing worldwide expansion of capital" and seen as being "the only realistic alternative [since] reform of the [present] world system is utopian." In his view, "history shows us that it is impossible to 'catch up' within the framework of world capitalism"; in fact, "only a very long transition" (with a self-conscious choice for delinking from the world of capitalist globalization as an essential first step) beyond the present global polarization will suffice.

16 I first cited Thomas' formulation in Saul, *The Next Liberation Struggle* (*op. cit.*), p. 51 and also evoked it to complement Amin's concept of "delinking" in my "Is Socialism Still an Alternative?" in *Studies in Political Economy*, #86 (Autumn).

the dilemma that has heretofore undermined the promise of the many "socialisms" which have then proven prone to falling into the Stalinist trap of "violently repressing mass consumption." For, far from accumulation and mass consumption being warring opposites, the premise would then be that accumulation could be driven forward precisely by finding outlets for production in meeting the growing requirements, the needs, of the mass of the population!

An effective industrialization strategy would thus base its "expanded reproduction" on ever increasing exchanges between city and country, between industry and agriculture, with food and raw materials moving to the cities and with consumer goods and producer goods (the latter defined to include centrally such modest items as scythes, iron ploughs, hoes, axes, fertilizers and the like) moving to the countryside. Collective saving geared to investment could then be seen as being drawn essentially, if not exclusively, from an expanding economic pool. Note that such a socialism of expanded reproduction makes the betterment of the people's lot a short-term rather than a long-term project and thus promises a much sounder basis for an effective (rather than merely rhetorical) alliance of workers, peasants and others – on a democratic road to revolutionary socialism.[17]

But this is, of course, precisely an emphasis that Nyerere and company turned their backs on. Thus Bill Luttrell,[18] writing quite explicitly within the framework established by Thomas, demonstrates the almost complete failure of the "bureaucratic class" in Tanzania to do so, their continued subservience to the logic of global capitalism ensuring their long-term failure to actually develop the country. He then spells out an alternative track that might have been taken had the elite really wanted to pursue transformation. Moreover, while Luttrell says little about Nyerere himself, another crucial missing link – industrial strategy (to be added to silences

17 This position is also spelled out at greater length in my "Is Socialism Still an Alternative?," (*ibid.*).

18 William L. Luttrell, *Post-Capitalist Industrialization: Planning Economic Independence in Tanzania* (New York: Praeger, 1986).

about democracy and failures of imagination in the rural sector) – in Nyerere's presumed socialist strategy here stands starkly exposed.

There are other fronts upon which to locate such a critical perspective. Thus, as noted earlier,[19] in discussing students as a "social category" of potentially radical provenance, Michelle Borbonniere concludes her account of the early years at the University by suggesting that "the Akivaga crisis, which was seen as a failure to follow through on the promise of *Mwongozo* at the university, was the first indication of a gap between Nyerere's political theory and practice." And what of women, the entire sphere of struggle for gender emancipation and gender equality? This was a front of "liberation" little discussed at the time in Tanzania, and, indeed, the record was not an encouraging one. For example, Bibi Titi, admittedly no great socialist but a prominent TANU leader in the early days, underscored some years ago the starkness of the male sense of entitlement that marked TANU in those years, the vital role of women militants in the liberation struggle itself soon being more or less passed over.

> When power was transferred to the nationalist government...the story changed. Women's experience was no longer relevant to the postcolonial struggles against neo-colonialism, imperialism and the management of the state apparatus. In [our] discussion Bibi Titi ironically said, "I started smelling fish" when the first cabinet was named.[20]

Indeed, so incensed by this was Bibi Titi that, by her account, she actually refused Nyerere's offer to co-author with him a joint history of Tanzania's nationalist liberation struggle! Meanwhile, the prevailing silences of that time have continued to scar present-day reality in Tanzania, despite the best efforts of many women activists then and now to keep the struggle for gender emancipation alive.

19   Borbonniere, *op. cit.*, p. 146.

20   Ruth Meena, "A Conversation with Bibi Titi: A Political Veteran" in Marjorie Mbilinyi, Mary Rusimbi, Chachage S. L. Chachage, and Demere Kiyunga (ed.), *Activist Voices: Feminist Struggles for an Alternative World* (Dar es Salaam: Tanzania Gender Networking Programme, 2003), p. 152. The interview with Bibi Titi, on which this article focusses was carried out by Ms. Meena in 1988.

* * *

Strengths and weaknesses, then. But the question remains: should not Tanzania's socialist moment constitute a very real learning experience for a continent that has still not fully confronted the threat of continuing subordination by global capital (including in its present-day Chinese form)? A lot depends, of course, on what you wish to learn. But in a very real sense one is tempted to say that *nothing* has been learned – or, if something has indeed been "learned," it has been entirely the wrong thing. Thus, in South Africa, to take one example, the latter is precisely the case. There, the cases of Tanzania and Mozambique have been viewed, particularly by that country's black elite, entirely one-sidedly and quite opportunistically – as having been, quite simply, case-studies of misguided policies, case-studies of, precisely, what *not to do*.[21]

In short: not to attempt to realize socialism but instead to settle for a virtual recolonization by global capital! For, the truth is that the lesson actually taken has been *not to dare*: not to dare to challenge such capital, not to dare to challenge local hierarchies, not to dare to critique fundamentally the presumed logic of the market-place. But is this really what Africa should learn from Tanzania? No, I would suggest, the lesson could be quite a different one: the very real costs of not to have dared *enough*. Indeed, with respect to this issue posed in this way, the jury is surely still out. The deeper problems and challenges that existed in the 1960s and 1970s continue to confront Africa today. They had begun to be sketched by Nyerere and the early TANU leadership, as they had been earlier by Nkrumah (for all the weaknesses of his own project), by Cabral and Fanon, and later by the likes of Eduardo Mondlane and Samora Machel.

Yet the fact also remains that in Tanzania there still reside many of the poorest of the continent's (and the world's) poor, the failed promise of

---

21   See, on this question, my "Socialism and Southern Africa," in Michelle Williams and Vishwas Satgar, eds., *Introducing New Approaches to Marxism: Critique and Struggle* (Johannesburg: Wits University Press, forthcoming).

the Arusha Years, long since a distant memory but mocking the present nonetheless. In consequence, the experience of Nyerere, the Mwalimu, continues – warts and all – to have much to teach us: in its aspirations and its praxis, for better and for worse. Whether, either in Tanzania or elsewhere on the continent, Africans can or will choose – any more effectively than the rest of us around the world have done in parallel situations of unfulfilled dreams and unrealized possibilities – to learn from such experience to take up with ever greater effectiveness the struggle, and to confront successfully a sobering post-colonial legacy in order to overcome it, these remain open questions.

CHAPTER 3

Mozambique – not Then but Now[1]

I first knew Mozambique through close contact in Dar es Salaam with Frelimo in the early and difficult years – the 1960s and the first-half of the 1970s – of its armed liberation struggle. At that time Mozambique was seeking both to unite itself and to find political and military purchase against an intransigent and arrogant Portuguese colonialism. And Frelimo did indeed manage, by 1975, to lead the country to victory. Along the way, Frelimo succeeded in liberating zones in Mozambique adjacent to its rear bases in Tanzania and Zambia where it built a new social infrastructure of agricultural co-ops, schools and health services. Equally important, it forged an impressive corps of politically conscious and disciplined leadership cadres.[2]

Then, in the very first years of Mozambique's independence, Frelimo also launched a bold experiment in socialist development. The intention:

---

1   This essay, in much the same form, was first published in the symposium on southern Africa cited in chapter 1, footnote 1.

2   José-Luis Cabaço, "THE NEW MAN (Brief Itinerary of a Project)," in A. Sopa, ed. *Samora: a Man of the People*, (Maputo: Maguezo Editores, 2001), pp. 103–110, and also José-Luis Cabaço, *Moçambique: identidade, colonialismo e libertaçao* (Saø Paolo: Editora UNESP, 2009).

to implement a society-wide programme that would liberate the country's economic potential while also meeting the needs of the vast majority of Mozambique's population. The result? As Norrie MacQueen would firmly state of former "Portuguese Africa," the initial plans of Portugal's "guerrilla enemies" did offer "a clear alternative to the cynical manipulation of ethnicity and the neo-colonial complaisance of the kleptocratic elites who increasingly defined African governance in the 1970s and 1980s." In sum:

> Whatever their fate, the projects of the post-independence regimes of lusophone Africa were probably the most principled and decent ever proposed for the continent. They have not been superseded in this regard and seem unlikely to be.[3]

This seems to me[4] to have been especially true of the new Mozambique during its first heroic decade of independence. Equally dramatic, however, has been the reversal of direction that has taken place in the country since that time. For what we have now witnessed, in Alice Dinerman's words, is nothing less than a "rapid unravelling of the Mozambican revolution," with the result that Mozambique, once considered a virtually peerless pioneer in forging a socialist pathway in Africa, "now enjoys an equally exceptional, if dialectically opposed, status: today the country is, in the eyes of the IMF and the World Bank, a flagship of neoliberal principles." Moreover, as Dinerman concludes:

> Predictably, many of the leading government and party officials rank among the primary beneficiaries of the new political and economic dispensation. Those who enthusiastically promised that Mozambique would turn into a graveyard of capitalism are now the leading advocates of, and avid accumulators in, capitalism's recent, full-blown resurrection.[5]

3   Norrie MacQueen, *The Decolonization of Portuguese Africa: Metropolitan Revolution and the Dissolution of Empire* (Harlow: Longman, 1997), pp. 236–237.

4   See the relevant sections of my *Revolutionary Traveller* (*op. cit.*).

5   Alice Dinerman, *Revolution, Counter-revolution and Revisionism in Post-colonial Africa: the Case of Mozambique* (Milton Park and New York: Routledge, 2006), pp. 19–20.

There are a number of possible explanations for such an outcome, and commentators (including the present author) have continued endlessly to debate their relative weight and significance. Certainly the country's inheritance from colonial domination was a poor one, reflected in such weaknesses as the paucity of trained indigenous personnel and in an economic dependence that pulled the country strongly towards subordination to global dictate despite efforts to resist it. There was also the ongoing regional war that made Mozambique the target of destructive incursions by white-dominated Rhodesia and South Africa and of the long drawn-out campaign of terror waged so callously and destructively by these countries' sponsored ward, the Renamo counter-revolutionary movement. Finally, and despite Frelimo's benign intentions, there were the movement's own sins once in power, sins of vanguardist high-handedness and impatience and of the over-simplification of societal complexities and challenges. The latter weaknesses created additional obstacles of their own to further progress.

The results, in fact, have been bleak. For what now occurred, Bauer and Taylor suggest, was the extremely rapid growth and dramatic spread of corruption (more or less unknown in the initial days of Independence) in Mozambique, as well as a fevered "pursuit of individual profit [that has undermined] much of the legitimacy of Frelimo party leaders, who [have taken] advantage of market-based opportunities, like privatization, to enrich themselves." In short, as these authors then also observe:

> the election of Guebuza [as the new President in 2002, and since], holder of an expansive business network and one of the richest men in Mozambique, hardly signals that Frelimo will attempt to run on anything but a globalist, neoliberal agenda – regardless of the abject poverty suffered by most of its electorate.[6]

Such a sombre conclusion seems to many observers an all too accurate one, unfortunately.

---

6   Bauer and Taylor (*op. cit.*, pp. 134–135).

Here, however, the main task of this chapter comes clearly into focus: what is the nature of the present "globalist, neoliberal agenda"? What kind of prospects, if any, does it promise for the country? What alternatives to it exist, concretely? For it is much too late in the day for an essay like the present one to stop at "mere" historical investigation or to preoccupy itself with the task of post-mortem and "might-have-beens." Rather we must carefully assess the actually existing moment in present-day Mozambique – while also seeking cautiously to divine the future. This is no small challenge, as we will see.

For there are a number of competing paradigms that are proposed in order to shape any such assessment. One, quite straightforwardly, sees the current unapologetically capitalist project as marking a promising revival of sobriety in Mozambique. Here, at last (or so it is argued by elites both global and local), is an acceptance by Frelimo and by the country it governs of the beneficent logic of global capitalism and the slow but certain working of the system's developmental magic. And certain figures as to growth rate are generally cited to support this claim: for example, a report from the UNDP's International Poverty Centre in 2007 quotes a growth rate for the preceding year of 7.9 percent, a rather impressive figure![7]

Yet the report also states this kind of growth rate – like similar statistics that are said to signal the country's socio-economic progress since the end of the country's wasting war in 1992 and the linked introduction of ever more accelerated "free market" reforms – to be "illusory at best."[8] As it affirms, "most of the growth in income and consumption actually occurred among the population's richest quintile, with less than 10 per-

---

7   This report, itself readily available, is summarised in the article "Mozambique: What price the benefits of foreign investment?" (UN-IRIN [United Nations Integrated Regional Information Network] Report of 2007, entitled "Mozambique 2007") This is available at <http://www.mopanetree.com/business- economy/4475-mozambique-what-price-benefits-foreign-investment.html> [accessed 1 May 2009].

8   From paragraph 5 of *ibid.* ("Mozambique: What price the benefits of foreign investment?").

cent of the growth affecting the country's poorest." Indeed, in the United Nations' 2007/2008 Human Development Index, the country still ranked 172 out of the 177 countries listed.

Two linked dimensions of this apparent growth stand out starkly here. First is the inescapable fact of the deep and widespread poverty thus alluded to. For even if some of the results in "growth" terms can seem mathematically positive, the national development and poverty reduction dividends of this impressive growth rate are virtually absent. In fact, the reality in terms of extreme maldistribution and its impact on people's lives is most distressing. Hanlon[9] gives a particularly clear account of the social distemper which desperate poverty and hunger has produced in both the rural and urban spaces, and he documents the panic and rage of the poor as "local people make a desperate attempt to regain some power – as a disempowered group finally taking a stand to defend its very survival."[10]

True, the organized working class does retain some space to negotiate better wages and working conditions and otherwise act to defend itself. Unions are able to operate freely and workers are able to choose whether or not to join a union. Central labour bodies have formed a "concertation" structure for acting upon issues of common interest and to participate in national policy discussions around public policy questions like establishment of minimum wage levels and changes in the labour law. Some unions, of the security guards for example, have acted especially militantly, taking wage and hours of work issues to labour tribunals and undertaking strike actions in the face of companies like the large transnational security

---

9   See, *inter alia*, Joe Hanlon, 2007. "Mozambique: the war ended 15 years ago, but we are still poor," a country case study prepared for "Conflict Prevention and Development Cooperation in Africa: A Policy Workshop," 2007; Joe Hanlon, "Mozambique: the panic and rage of the poor," *Review of African Political Economy*, 36, #119 (2009), pp. 125–130 and B. Cuanguara and Joe Hanlon, "Poverty is not being reduced in Mozambique," Working Paper 24, (London: London School of Economics Crisis States Research Centre, 2010).

10 Hanlon, "Mozambique: the panic and rage of the poor" (*ibid.*), p. 129.

company, G4S, which has flagrantly refused to follow Ministry of Labour rulings in the union's favour.[11]

This being said, however, the space for workers' challenges still remains severely limited, not only because of the structural factors that favour capital's interests but also because the trade unions themselves seem to have too little sense of workers' entitlements[12] – this in a context where, as Pitcher states with impressive supportive citations, any apparent concessions to such workers must be balanced against "the reality of growing unemployment; a minimum wage that is insufficient to meet people's needs; and inadequate efforts by the government to enforce aspects of the labour law regarding paid holidays, the regular payment of salaries and the punishment of employers who violate workers' rights."[13]

A second dimension is the clear pattern of recolonization by global capital of the new Mozambique that is revealed. For the present salience of transnational firms and their "mega-projects" – on which the Mozambican elite has itself banked so heavily, not least in order to obtain lucrative subcontracts for their own fledgling economic initiatives – virtually negates

---

11 Interestingly, some of the staunchest defence of workers' rights in recent years has come not from the unions but from the Frelimo Minister of Labour, Helena Taipo. Acting on her own conviction that the role of the government is to maintain balance and mutual respect amongst the main actors in the economy, she has intervened on multiple occasions where workers' rights have not been respected, coming down hard on employers ranging from large transnationals like the G4S security company and Mozal, to Chinese state companies and senior government leaders turned businessmen.

12 True, the unions themselves sometimes seem to act in such a way as to mediate labour conflicts away rather than to take a militant stand for workers' rights to a living wage, a safe workplace and dignified treatment. Moreover, many workers seem to read the strong government support for new mega-projects like those of BHP-Billiton and Vale and the modest government role in defending those whose lands and livelihoods are lost to these projects as an indication that fighting these companies for better wages and working conditions is almost tantamount to anti-government activity.

13 Anne Pitcher, "Forgetting from above and memory from below: strategies of legitimation and struggle in postsocialist Mozambique," *Africa*, 76, 1 (2006), p. 105.

the presumed independence that "liberation" was said to have brought. The case of Mozal is a particularly graphic demonstration of the pattern, an aluminium plant that is said to be "a symbol of Mozambique's red-hot economy, touted as [indicative] of the investor-friendly environment that has led the *Wall Street Journal* to declare the country 'An African success story.' Mozal's exports have increased Mozambique's Gross Domestic Product by between 3.2 and 5 percent. Its output represents almost half the country's growth in manufacturing." However, as this article in the *Wall Street Journal* continues,

> In spite of these apparent benefits this has contributed little to the country's development. Initial investment in the project amounted to approximately 40 percent of GDP, but only created around 1,500 jobs, of which nearly a third are held by foreigners. The smelters use more electricity than the rest of Mozambique combined. The company imports most of its raw material and equipment duty-free, and enjoys an extensive list of incentives ranging from discounted electricity to a prolonged tax holiday. It also has the right to repatriate profits. The result is an isolated economic enclave that uses large quantities of scarce resources without returning revenue or jobs to the economy.[14]

Castel-Branco and Pitcher[15] document similar patterns, linked to mega-projects and to corporate free-booting, elsewhere throughout the

---

14 In "Mozambique: What price the benefits of foreign investment?" (*op. cit.*)

15 See C. N. Castel-Branco, "Desafios do desenvolvimento rural em Moçambique: contributo critico com debate de postulados basicos," Discussion paper #3/2008. Maputo: Colleçao de Discussion Papers de IESE [Instituto de Estudos Sociais e Economicos, 2008]; C. N. Castel-Branco, "Os mega projectos em Moçambique: que contributo para a economia nacional?" Paper presented to the Forum da Sociedade Civil sobre Industria Extractiva, Museu de História Natural, Maputo, 27–28 November 2008; and Pitcher, *op. cit.* See also Noaman Ali, *Frelimo and the political economy of Mozambique, 1975–2008* (Toronto: York University Department of Political Science, 2009); Luis de Brito, et. al., "Reflecting...2008"; and de Brito, et al., "Reflecting on economic questions and Southern Africa and challenges for Mozambique," Papers from the Inaugural Conference of the Institute for Social and Economic Studies in September, 2007 (Maputo: IESE, 2008); and Brito, L. de, et al., "Desafios para Mozambique 2010," Papers from the Inaugural Conference of the Institute for Social and Economic Studies in September, 2007 (Maputo: IESE, 2009).

Mozambican economy. Pitcher, for example, specifies the case of CFM (Portos e Caminhos de Moçambique), a public enterprise in the port and railways sector that was, until recently, "the largest employer in Mozambique" and where management has sought aggressively "to rationalize the work-force" and make other kinds of adjustments thought to be appropriate to the new era – albeit, as with related practices that Pitcher also demonstrates for Mozal, this has not occurred without some attempted resistance from the workers concerned.

Meanwhile, Judith Marshall finds an even rawer example of the nature of the "new Mozambique" in the key role being played by the giant Brazilian multinational, Vale, in a range of big mining, hydroelectric and transport projects in Tete Province. This is both central to the heralding (not least by President Guebuza himself) of a "Tete Corridor" initiative, but also of a new "high octane global economy that feeds China's industrialization and in which Vale's role is [to provide] unprocessed minerals."[16] And what about Mozambique? All this, Marshall concludes, "has nothing to do with building a national economy – whether socialist or capitalist – or creating jobs and development for the citizens of a particular geo-political space."[17] Recolonization by the Empire of Capital you say: you would not be wrong if you did.[18]

In practice, Mozambique seems to have come up with a two-pillar development strategy. The first pillar is to open the economy to private in-

---

16   On Vale's egregious role in Canada, since 2006 the owner of Inco (now Vale Inco), see B. Evans and Greg Albo, "Celebrating and struggling this May Day: the long, hard haul at the Vale Inco strike," *The Bullet* (The Socialist Project E-Bulletin), 349 (May 1, 2010).

17   Judith Marshall, personal communication. Here and elsewhere in this text Marshall's advice and assistance have been particularly important to its preparation, helping me to ground it firmly in contemporary reality. Comments from both Noaman Ali (see also Ali 2009) and Jesse Ovadia have also been of great assistance, as have recent writings by Luis de Brito (2008 and 2009).

18   For more on these concepts, see chapter 1, above, and also John S. Saul, *Liberation Lite* (*op. cit.*).

vestors to bring mega-projects to the energy and extractive sectors. These mega-projects are driven by the external demands of the industrialised countries, and include the active roles played by capital from countries like South Africa, Brazil and China – with the role of the Mozambican state, the corporations themselves and civil society in these new projects being highly problematic, as Marshall and others demonstrate.

Moreover, such mega-projects have come on stream as merely one part of the tide of neo-liberal economic and social restructuring. As a result, they are very far from feeding into a strategy of national economic development, one that might highlight job creation and links to plans for expanded industrialization – with royalties and taxes then being employed to benefit the surrounding communities and to underpin a broad range of social and redistributive programmes. Instead, they have been established in a way that implicitly negates the possibility of any kind of genuinely nationalist or effectively developmental state emerging.

Indeed, such an influx of mega-projects in the extractive sector suggests an overall trend in Mozambique that has come to mirror what has also been happening with the "mining boom" in Latin America.[19] All kinds of conditions are being created to attract foreign private investment – from tax holidays to changes in mining and labour codes, to the waiving of environmental regulations. Of course, much public discourse turns on "corporate social responsibility" and on the promise of mining-company largesse for the building of schools, clinics, roads and malaria eradication. Yet, behind the scenes, high stakes negotiations turn on tax and tariff waivers, changes in land, mining and labour legislation, the easing of environmental regulations and a distinctly casual attitude towards forced human resettlement. The stakes in these less than transparent negotiations are all the higher in that the complementary business opportunities

19   In the original I included here in a footnote an extensive reference to Liisa North et al., *Community Rights and Corporate Responsibility* (Toronto: Between the Lines, 2006) on very related experience in Latin America that is well worth looking at.

related to these mega-project investments seem all too likely to be linked to the entrepreneurial interests of various government leaders.

With mega-projects in the extractive sector as one pillar of Mozambique's economic strategy, the other pillar of the national economy, much documented by Hanlon, is defined by Mozambique's having become a "donors' darling": a country that, as an apparent reward for its eager compliance with International Monetary Fund (IMF) and World Bank prescriptions and the periodic holding of multi-party elections (albeit with some donor concern about "irregularities" in their execution), receives significant amounts of foreign aid in order to finance social programmes. Of course, this has even produced a significant role for the state – linked to the provision of agriculture, health and education services – albeit one heavily subsidized by Western donors.

The more cynical suggest that, even were quite modest levels of taxes and royalties demanded of investors, the Mozambican government could itself readily finance all the social programmes that it desired. Yet it chooses to establish no such taxes and royalties and to suffer instead the indignity of Western donors who hover at the elbows of the Ministers of Health, Agriculture and Education. In fact, this pattern – low taxes, little government oversight – seems designed to clinch investment deals while also permitting government leaders to ingratiate themselves with investors, thereby laying the groundwork for such leaders, in their entrepreneurial capacity, to then seal lucrative private partnerships. Meanwhile, foreign donors wind up funding social costs: in such a way Canadian taxpayers – and those in other donor countries – find themselves subsidizing transnational mining companies in Mozambique![20]

---

20   The previous several paragraphs draw heavily on the suggestions and formulations of Judith Marshall, as cited in footnote 17, above. She further notes that even "the donors" began to become uneasy with the Mozambican elite's behaviour. Thus "the beginning of 2010 found these arrangements fraying at the edges. The donors delayed their transfers to the social ministries until such time as the Mozambican government was prepared to introduce changes in its electoral law and regulations regarding conflict of interest" (personal communication).

Are there countervailing trends to these disturbing patterns – and ways of interpreting them – that bear more promise? As seen, Hanlon is both a clear-sighted observer of the cruel inequality between elite and mass that has come to mark contemporary Mozambique and has also been a sharp critic of the overall multinationals-driven economic strategy championed by the country's elite in recent decades. Nonetheless, Hanlon's more recent work provides a sharply contrasting point of reference against which to underscore the present argument.

For he seems now to have come to a rather startling conclusion. As he and his co-author Teresa Smart put it, "in the contemporary world, development tends to be capitalist in some form."[21] Hence they endorse the view of President Guebuza that, in their own words, "Mozambique cannot wait with hands outstretched for mythical foreign investors, but must create, support and promote its own business people" – people, it bears emphasising, like President Guebuza himself and other such members of Mozambique's fledgling national bourgeoisie!

In fact, in recent writings Hanlon professes to discern the transformation of the latter Mozambicans from an erstwhile elite of robber barons (identified as such in his earlier texts) into captains of industry, and he makes a strong (and, for him, novel) case for the developmental vocation of just such a "national bourgeoisie." Thus, with Mosse, he asks, startlingly, whether "Mozambique's elite [is] moving from corruption to development."[22] In another recent article he sees that elite to be "finding its way in a globalized economy."[23] In such articles, he explores, revealingly,

---

21   Joe Hanlon and Teresa Smart, *Do Bicycles Equal Development in Mozambique?* (Woodbridge, Suffolk: James Currey, 2008), p. 3.

22   Joe Hanlon and Marcelo Mosse, "Is Mozambique's elite moving from corruption to development," UNU-WIDER Conference on the Role of Elites in Economic Development, Helsinki, Finland, 12–13 June, 2009), p. 1.

23   Joe Hanlon, "Mozambique's elite – finding its way in a globalized world and returning to old development models," paper presented at London School of Economics, Crisis States Research Centre, October. Also available as United Nations University (UNU) World Institute for Development Economics Research (WIDER) Working

the precise make-up of this elite and the wide range of their various hold-ing and economic interests. Writing with Mosse, for example, he places particular emphasis on the role of the President and the "Guebuza family companies," noting Guebuza's aggressive business sense and the roots of their present practice in the degree to which he and other key members of the elite (former President Joaquim Chissano for example) have built on bases derived from their stake in the "gangster capitalism," and "greed is good" days, of the 1990s when they were able "to expand their interests under the party and state umbrella."[24]

The list of the holdings of Guebuza, his immediate family and other relatives (and of other close associates like Celso Correia), is quite stag-gering. But the Guebuza group is also distinguished, says Hanlon, by a less "predatory," more "developmental," approach than many others of the elite – something he sees to be most promising. Recall that Hanlon was once amongst those who had effectively excoriated that very Mo-zambican elite as it became, over time, more and more visibly corrupt and opportunist in the seizing of all manner of market opportunities. Now such is Hanlon's attraction to Guebuza's charisma, to his national-ism, and to his savvy, that, by means of his (Hanlon's) authorial magic, Mozambique's robber baron elite is, as I have suggested, suddenly to emerge as captains of industry – and conjurors of genuine development! Indeed, the key question Hanlon and Mosse now wish to pose seems to be whether the development of presidential companies should be more openly encouraged as a way of creating firms and groups which are dy-namic and effective enough to be competitive and developmental. Can these presidential companies through their privileged access to the state potentially grow to a critical mass allowing them to become major players in the development of Mozambique and southern Africa, as happened with the privileged companies in the Asian Tigers, Latin America and South

---

Paper No. 2010/105. Helsinki: UNU-WIDER.

24   See footnote 22, above.

Africa? And, Hanlon and Mosse further ask, can "the Mozambican elite" not also "develop the culture of hard work, saving and delayed consumption that was central to the economic development of the Asian Tigers."[25]

But, even if some such transformation were to occur, to whose benefit would it actually be in any case? To the "robber-barons'" own, self-evidently. And what of the impoverished mass of the population? It would surely take a pretty powerful "trickle-down effect" to see Mozambique move up from number 172 on the world table to be able to establish any convincing comparison with the Asian Tigers as Hanlon implies to be possible. Nonetheless, this kind of capitalist transformation, driven by just this kind of indigenous bourgeoisie, seems to be the best scenario, the best hope, that Hanlon can conjure up for Mozambique and for Mozambicans.

Is this where the experience of both the failure of Mozambique's socialism and the subsequent recolonization – both socially damaging and, in any transformative sense, economically unsuccessful – of the country by global capitalism must drive the well-intentioned observer: into the arms of the country's local elite who have, in fact, themselves been amongst the chief architects of the country's present sorry situation? Make no mistake here. Hanlon is massively well informed and also cares deeply about Mozambique, about its prospects for genuine development, and about the fate of its numberless poor. But would it not be possible for him and for us, instead, to look downwards, to the impoverished populace itself, instead of upwards, to the indigenous would-be bourgeoisie, for any real promise of realising fair and meaningful change? In sharp contrast to Hanlon's latest vision, at once nationalist and bourgeois, there remains a final scenario to be considered, a prospect that pins its hopes on a revival of the country's progressive vocation.

Is this any less fanciful and fugitive a hope than is Hanlon's? Certainly the immediate prospects along these progressive lines are not great. Yet Anne Pitcher – though herself well aware of the growing wealth and power

---

25   *Ibid.*, p. 10.

that the Mozambican elite is creating for itself – can still talk hopefully about the negative impact of elite self-aggrandizement on the attitudes and actions of those many millions of citizens, abandoned and often quite desperate, who seem consigned to languish "at the bottom" and well "below" the status and comfort afforded those at the top of Mozambican society.[26]

Indeed, she goes further, suggesting a particularly tantalising way of thinking about this reality. On the one hand, Pitcher finds that the elite is busily rewriting history and recasting its public pronouncements (in ways she documents extremely clearly) so as to block any popular recall – especially any positive recall – of an earlier socialist and progressive Frelimo. Yet, she continues, the ordinary Mozambicans are not so easily convinced, sickened by and angry at the dramatically escalating corruption and rampant greed they see to be everywhere around them in the "new Mozambique" – while also both holding on to their own memories of a more promising time and manifesting their continued expectations of a state that protects its citizens.

Pitcher places more hope than may be warranted in the Mozambican trade unions perhaps, some of whose weaknesses we noted above. Nonetheless, she does forcefully argue the importance of widespread worker protests that centre on demands for "benefits and subsidies that the government guaranteed to them in the past." And she also emphasises the importance of other realities like

> the robust sales of the recorded speeches of President Samora Machel, who oversaw the implementation of socialism from 1977 until his death in 1986 [that] reveal an ongoing popular dissatisfaction with the current mode of governance and lingering attachments to another time.[27]

Moreover, it is the case that industries in the extractive sector – some of which, as in mining, also have an insatiable appetite for land – often find themselves increasingly to be in conflict with rural communities. Indeed,

---

26   Pitcher, *op. cit.*

27   Pitcher, *ibid.*, p. 106.

with the withdrawal of the state from regulating and protecting its citizens' rights, the companies and such communities are actually advancing quite different and competing visions of development! Local demands for job creation, for localised control of new business opportunities such as transport, food services and security, for adequate compensation to those displaced, for environmental protection of water sources, and the like: around each of these issues there is the likelihood of growing resistance.[28]

In fact, drawing on recent evidence of protests, strikes and other instances of overt resistance in present-day Mozambique, Pitcher concludes that, even if a recent letter of protest (which she quotes) to the editor of *Noticias* in Maputo may be "somewhat romantic about the good old days, it [does show] that a counter-hegemonic strategy rooted in socialist ideals may be (re-)emerging in Mozambique." Aiming not so much, it would seem, to revive Frelimo's original project as to imagine the possibility of recasting the present in order that it might again embody something that will be (for them) much more positive. Grasping at straws? Note that this sometime populist strain of resistance to penury and oppression can often be randomly violent, xenophobic and malfocused, as Hanlon has emphasised. Moreover, it is, even in its very best expressions, still a long way from embodying the principled and organised force for change that could expect soon to present an alternative – and winning – counter-hegemonic "strategy" (such as Pitcher evokes) to the Frelimo elite's now self-indulgent and largely self-serving rule. Yet perhaps it can at least be said that, at the present grim time in Mozambique, the struggle for a more genuine liberation is far from being wholly moribund.

---

28 For there is also the promising fact that transnational mining companies are not the only players that have begun to establish complex multinational linkages: civil-society networks concerned with mining issues are also connected. Indeed, as the African experience comes to mirror that of Asia and South America where these kinds of new mining investments are more advanced, Mozambican organizations will, in all likelihood, soon be sharing even more experiences and strategies with other communities in resistance around the world.

Chapter 4
On Taming a Revolution
The South African Case[1]

Any sober strategy for realizing progressive, let alone socialist, goals from the promising drama of the new struggles emerging in South Africa must necessarily begin with an interrogation of South Africa's disappointing path to the present.[2] Such an interrogation must, of course, be done with care. As emphasized earlier, one does not want to trivialize in any way that which, with the overthrow of apartheid, has been accomplished: the

---

1 This essay was first published, in more or less the same form, in Leo Panitch, Greg Albo and Vivek Chibber (eds.), *The Socialist Register 2013* (London: Merlin Press, 2012); its inclusion here affords the opportunity to correct a grievous error in the earlier essay where Saul allowed a confusion between two estimable authors on South Africa, Eleanor Jean Wood and Allison Drew (editor of the two volume work, cited in this text, and entitled *South Africa's Radical Tradition: a Documentary History* [Cape Town: Buchu Books, Mayibuye Books and the University of Cape Town Press, 1996/7]) to slip in, assigning Wood's book *Forging Democracy from Below* (Cambridge: Cambridge University Press, 2000) to Drew! I apologize to both writers for the original mistake. This essay also served to structure and indeed to lend a number of its specific formulations to chapter 2, "In Struggle: The Transition to a New South Africa, 1960-1994," of John S. Saul and Patrick Bond, *South Africa – The Present as History* (*op. cit.*) where some of the arguments presented here are given further elaboration and documentation.

2 For an examination of these more current struggles see my chapter 7, entitled "Liberating Liberation: The Struggle Against Recolonization in South Africa," in Saul and Bond (*ibid.*) and also the very different chapter 6 of the present book as well.

defeat of a bankrupt and evil system of institutionalized racism, a system entirely worthy of its consignment to the global scrapheap of history. Yet in what now looks like a classic case study of how to demobilize a potential revolution, the African National Congress (ANC), working with its new allies, both domestic and foreign, has succeeded in integrating South Africa firmly into the broader world of global capitalism.

As South Africa entered its key transition years (from the mid-1980s to the mid-1990s) it would have been hard to imagine that a bald swap of apartheid for the country's recolonization within the newly ascendant Empire of Capital could ever be seen as being a very impressive accomplishment.[3] Yet it is just such an outcome that has occurred in South Africa, one that has produced – alongside some minimal narrowing of the economic gap between black and white (as a result, primarily, of a small minority of blacks moving up the income ladder) – both a marked widening of the gap between rich and poor (the latter mainly black) and a failure to realize any substantial progress towards tangible "development" and meaningful popular empowerment. It is precisely this recolonization of South Africa, occurring on the ANC's watch, that forms the context within which the left in that country now seeks to regroup and to struggle.

In this chapter, then, we are left to pose some sobering questions about the country's very transition away from apartheid: what kind of liberation has really occurred in South Africa anyway? How has what happened been allowed to happen? And how has the ANC managed, thus far, to get away with it?

1. Biko and Beyond

The key to understanding this denouement was, in fact, provided in a deftly illuminating commentary by none other than Steve Biko. Asked, in 1972, to reflect on the economy of the country, and identify "what trends

---

3   On the concepts both of "recolonization" and of a new "Empire of Capital" – one not so readily defined as previously in terms of various nationally-defined imperial purposes – see, again, my *Decolonization of Empire* (*op. cit.*).

or factors in it ... you feel are working towards the fulfillment of the long term ends of blacks," he suggested that the regime's deep commitment to a racial hierarchy had actually acted as "a great leveler" of class formation amongst the black population and dictated "a sort of similarity in the community" – such that the "constant jarring effect of the [apartheid] system" produced a "common identification" on the part of the people. Whereas, in the more liberal system envisaged by the Progressive Party of the time, "you would get stratification creeping in, with your masses remaining where they are or getting poorer, and the cream of your leadership, which is invariably derived from the so-called educated people, beginning to enter bourgeois ranks, admitted into town, able to vote, developing new attitudes and new friends ... a completely different tone." Indeed, South Africa is

> one country where it would be possible to create a capitalist black society, if the whites were intelligent. If the Nationalists were intelligent. And that capitalist black society, black middle-class, would be very effective at an important stage. Primarily because a hell of a lot of blacks have got a bit of education – I'm talking comparatively speaking to the so-called rest of Africa – and a hell of a lot of them could compete favorably with whites in the fields of industry, commerce and professions. And South Africa could succeed to put across to the world a pretty convincing integrated picture with still 70 percent of the population being underdogs.

Indeed, it was precisely because the whites were so "terribly afraid of this" that South Africa represented, to Biko, "the best economic system for revolution." For "the evils of it are so pointed and so clear, and therefore make teaching of alternative methods, more meaningful methods, more indigenous methods even, much easier under the present sort of setup."[4]

Needless to say, the Progressive Party of the 1970s was nowhere near power. And capitalists were, on the whole, still not nearly so reform-minded in the 1970s as Biko apparently felt the most enlightened of Progressive Party supporters then to be. In fact, the entire history of

---

4   Interview with Steve Biko, as carried out by Gail Gerhart on 24 October 1972, available at http://abahlali.org and from the Aluka e-collection of anti-apartheid-related materials at http://www.aluka.org.

twentieth century South Africa had been one much more defined by an alliance between racists and capitalists to ensure both racial and class advantage than one defined by any deep contradiction between the two camps. Flash forward to the late 1980s, however. The reform ("intelligent") wing of the National Party (NP) – together with those of the capitalist class, both of English and Afrikaner origin, who increasingly claimed the allegiance of NP reformers – had become just what Biko imagined the Progressive Party already to be in his own time.

For the NP was by then proving to be (at least at the top) a party capable – albeit with great caution and much obvious reluctance – of contemplating the shedding of apartheid for a system designed, more straightforwardly, both to empower a liberal capitalist regime and to move to facilitate black (even black majority) participation within it. For "intelligent racists" and capitalists alike could begin to see capital's link to the politics of racial domination as having been a contingent one. Not, needless to say, that the resultant transition to a (tendentially) colour-blind capitalism would be simple or entirely straightforward; there were genuinely dangerous alternative possibilities that had to be overcome. Nonetheless, the "false decolonization" evoked by Biko was to be, precisely, the ultimate outcome to which socialist strategy for South Africa in the twenty-first century would have to address itself.

Biko, in evoking the "Prog possibility," was of course following the analytical lead of Frantz Fanon. He had read and learned from Fanon's analysis of "successful" African nationalism across the northern and central portions of the continent as, in essence, fostering just such a "false decolonization" – this to the advantage of domestic and international capital and of the newly ascendant African elites.[5] Yet Biko's understanding of South Africa's quite specific possibilities was somewhat different. True, he was far from naive as regards the class dimensions of South

5   See, on this and many other related points, Lindi Wilson, *Steve Biko* (Auckland Park, S.A.: Jacana, 2011).

Africa's racial capitalism; indeed, Biko had good and fruitful relations in Durban with Rick Turner and others who would spark the reemergence of the working-class-based resistance that produced the urban strikes there (with increasingly important echoes across the country) in the early 1970s.[6]

Nonetheless, as Biko saw it, the racial structure of this system was what was central, and, for him, it was the emergence of a new confidence – and a more forthright 'black consciousness' – on the part of the mass of the country's oppressed black (African, Coloured and Indian) population that could most readily open the revolutionary door to a new South Africa. This, as we know, was the politics of black self-assertion that Biko himself would follow in the few years of life granted him by the apartheid regime. Nor can there be any doubt as to broad resonance of such a "black consciousness" emphasis – one evident in the events of Soweto (1976) and beyond – that helped fuel, throughout the 1970s and 1980s, a mass movement for dramatic change in South Africa.

2. The politics of the proletariat: The trade unions become COSATU

Yet it was working class action that surfaced first on the ground to express active resistance within the country in the 1970s. This new assertion was too class-based (rather than racially-based) to be unqualifiedly approved of by those of "black consciousness" sensibility. But it was also, in its orientation, much more specific and responsive to the immediate grievances of workers on the shop floor than was, for example, the South African Congress of Trade Unions (SACTU) – the latter's leadership now

---

6   Eddie Webster, oral communication and in his contributions to the public discussion following the presentation of his paper "A Seamless Web or a Democratic Rupture: The Re-Emergence of Trade Unions and the African National Congress (ANC) in Durban 1973 and Beyond," at the conference "One Hundred Years of the ANC: Debating Liberation Histories and Democracy Today," held in Johannesburg, 20–24 September 2011.

banned in any case and itself existing largely in exile as an international lobby group both within the global trade union network and as part of the ANC's own established alliance of organizations. SACTU's slant had been and continued to be (albeit now largely from exile rather than on the ground) the mobilization of workers for the broader purposes of "national liberation struggle."

But the worker assertions that emerged in Durban in the dramatic and novel shop-floor struggles in the early 1970s had a rather different perspective. The organizations being formed out of such industrial contestations sought tactically, and so as to escape excessive negative scrutiny by the apartheid state, to avoid any overly compromising links to the ANC/SACP/SACTU exile group. Many within the "new trade union movement" were also suspicious of such formations-in-exile, fearful, from the vantage point of their concern to safeguard worker interests and voice, of this exile triumvirate's vanguardist preoccupations and also its possible embrace of a negative, all-too Soviet/Stalinist modeled attitude towards true worker-centred empowerment from below.[7] Indeed, as Webster and Adler argue,

> the legal proscription of the nationalist movements meant that in their formative years [the] embryonic unions were able to develop leadership, organize their constituency, and define their strategies and tactics relatively independently from the ideological orientations and models of the ANC, SACP and especially their labour arm, SACTU. The space created by virtue of banning and exile meant that the new unions could develop innovative approaches to organizing that differed from the populist strategies and tactics of the nationalist-linked unions of the 1950s.[8]

In fact, the new labour activists of the seventies remained respectful of the SACTU tradition and of Congress history but without feeling unduly

7　I heard this position most forcibly articulated in the late seventies at their then shared house in Durban from both then trade union activists Alec Erwin and (at that time banned) Johnny Copleyn who ultimately came to move in quite different directions from the opinions they expressed on that earlier occasion.

8　Eddie Webster and Glenn Adler, "Exodus Without a Map: The Labour Movement in a Liberalizing South Africa," in Bjorn Beckman and L. M. Sachikonye, eds., *Labour Regimes and Liberalization: The Restructuring of State-Society Relations in Africa* (Harare: University of Zimbabwe Publications, 2001), p. 126.

beholden to them. Sparks struck by "shop-floor" confrontations at the Durban docks, the Coronation Brick and Tile Works, the Frame Group factories and at other sites in Durban quickly had dramatic resonance throughout the country as new trade union centrals surfaced (TUACC, FOSATU) and the wave of strike activity spread.[9] Indeed, a nationwide context was soon created within which, even as "labour movements throughout much of the world experienced declines in membership and influence during the 1980s and 1990s, the South African labour movement [grew] rapidly."[10]

Moreover, these unions were impressive manifestations of what Webster has termed "social movement unionism," for they were both fully conscious of the imperatives of the shop-floor struggles they launched while also being aware of the broader anti-apartheid resonance of their undertakings. Indeed, Joe Foster, the head of FOSATU, would make exactly this point in a widely-cited speech in the early 1980s:

> It is … essential that workers must strive to build their own powerful and effective organization even whilst they are part of the wider popular struggle. This organization is necessary to protect and further workers' interests and to ensure that the popular movement is not hijacked by elements who will in the end have no option but to turn against their worker supporters...[Indeed], in relation to the particular requirements of worker organization, mass parties and popular political organizations have definite limitations which have to be clearly understood by us.[11]

This was the emphasis that Bob Fine also underscored in introducing the republication of Foster's speech in the *Review of African Political Economy* at the time. There he drew a clear distinction between "popular

9   See, among other sources, The Institute for Industrial Education, *The Durban Strikes, 1973*, Durban: The Institute of Industrial Education, 1974; and Steven Friedman, *Building Tomorrow Today: African Workers in Trade Unions, 1970-1984*, Cape Town: Raven Press, 1987.

10   For more details on this see Webster and Adler, "Exodus Without a Map," p. 124; and Sakhela Buhlungu, *A Paradox of Victory: COSATU and the Democratic Transformation in South Africa*, Durban: University of Kwazulu-Natal Press, 2010.

11   See Foster's speech, published as "The Workers' Struggle: Where Does FOSATU Stand?," *Review of African Political Economy*, No. 24, 1982, pp. 99–114.

front" politics (where "the working class is merely wheeled in and out like
the crowd in a Shakespearean drama") and a much more assertive and effective working-class political presence, suggesting (already in 1982) that,
in contrast, "there are good reasons to believe that [the popular front] was
the basic conception behind the Congress Alliance; namely that SACTU
subordinated the specific interests and organization of workers first to
mass protest campaigns and then to the armed struggle."[12]

A clear warning for the future, perhaps. For the moment, however,
the initiatives of such new trade union centrals as TUAAC and FOSATU,
their seeds first sewn in Durban, increasingly moved centre stage, having,
as we shall see, profound impact both upon the capitalist class and the
apartheid state.[13] Indeed, the Wiehann Report of the later 1970s which
was to sanction the registration of African unions – albeit in the first instance the better to co-opt and control them – opened, in practice, space
for worker experimentation and ever more confident self-assertion. So
much so that FOSATU itself continued to spread, ultimately allying with
union initiatives of a quite different hue (these latter, like SACTU in its
time, being more "populist" – as the shorthand of the time had it – than
"workerist") but also with the crucially important National Union of
Mineworkers, to form, in December 1985, COSATU (the Confederation
of South African Trade Unions).

And COSATU was to remain a visible and active force of real
prominence throughout the 1980s. Indeed, when the crucial umbrella
organization of active community organizations, the United Democratic
Front (UDF, see below) was temporarily banned by the government in
1988, it was COSATU that sprang forward to take up the political slack,

12   Robert Fine, "The Workers' Struggle in South Africa," *Review of African Political
Economy*, No. 24, 1982, pp. 95–99.

13   Not that FOSATU and TUACC (the Federation of South African Trade Unions and
the Trade Union Advisory Coordinating Council) sounded the only emergent trade
union voices of black workers to be heard during this period, Webster and Adler
recording a number of other important initiatives of the time in their "Exodus
Without a Map," pp. 127–128.

anchoring the freshly minted "Mass Democratic Movement" that, for a period, took the UDF's place in coordinating the vast internal popular movement that fought back against the negation of resistance intended by the state's especially brutal response to the near revolution of the mid-1980s. Of course, it is also significant that the ANC, as it moved towards power at the turn of the nineties, did not – could not – adopt the same tactics towards COSATU that it was to use in facilitating the 1991 dissolution of the UDF. In the event, SACTU, the presumptive liberation movement trade union voice, was merely allowed, in 1990, to slip off the stage, its relative marginalization in exile from workers' struggles on the ground now tacitly acknowledged.

Nonetheless, COSATU had itself long sensed the need for a broader political project – one spearheading a counter hegemony to the historic hegemony of racial capitalism – that it could not readily imagine mounting alone. In this regard it grasped, as well, the seeming logic of its accepting the broader remit that the ANC was, during the transition period, increasingly claiming for itself. The decisive break with "political abstentionism" had come in November 1984 when FOSATU (very soon to also be a key actor in the formation of COSATU) entered into joint action with student and civic organizations to participate in the first successful worker stay-away since 1976. Then, only a few years later, "in one of their very first acts [after COSATU's own founding in late 1985], its new office bearers ... traveled to Lusaka and endorsed the ANC's leadership of the liberation struggle."[14]

True, there is little doubt that many within the COSATU camp failed to appreciate the fact that, even as the ANC and COSATU first met, the ANC was already in the process of refusing to countenance any counter-hegemonic perspectives whatsoever towards capitalism. For if COSATU was just too strong to be, like the UDF, merely removed from the scene, ultimately it was, in the 1990s, only to be permitted membership within

---

14   Webster and Adler, "Exodus Without a Map," p. 129.

a new ANC-SACP-COSATU alliance as a distinctly junior partner. Many of its own cadres would soon defect to jobs in party and state of course, while some momentary prospect (a false prospect, as it soon proved to be) of COSATU's playing an on-going transformative role could be thought to lie in the negotiations undertaken, with both business and state representatives, through the structures of the National Economic Development and Labour Council (NEDLAC).[15]

But there was also attrition of COSATU's own rank and file as the new ANC government's macroeconomic policies after 1994 saw both a decline in the number of stable jobs in industry and the emergence of an economy that would become ever more reliant on a part-time casual and insecure labour force.[16] Moreover, there was to be a growing number of workers in very precarious jobs (seasonal, temporary, casual or fixed-term contract work) – up to as many as 30 percent of the active labour force.[17] This latter group of workers also largely remains without trade union representation, with COSATU itself having as yet shown little vocation for organizing the unorganized. Indeed, it was tempting to see COSATU as becoming, in the post-apartheid period, increasingly representative of a "labour aristocracy" of the organized and better-paid workers. True, even if there is "more evidence for the concept's appropriateness now," the "labour aristocracy" label remains, as Webster warns, "misleading because neoliberal globalization is eroding the core of the labour market,

---

15 For a detailed discussion of the NEDLAC process, and more generally of the challenges facing COSATU during this period, see Carolyn Bassett, "Negotiating South Africa's Economic Future: COSATU and Strategic Unionism," a doctoral dissertation submitted to York University, 2000.

16 Indeed, Franco Barchiesi's (in his "Schooling Bodies to Hard Work: The South African State's Policy Discourse and Its Moral Constructions of Welfare," paper presented at the North Eastern Workshop on Southern Africa (NEWSA), Vermont, 2007) estimates that during the post-apartheid period "full time waged employment was a reality for only less than one third of the African economically active population."

17 As indicated by Marlea Clarke in a personal communication and in her "'All the Workers?': Labour Market Reform and 'Precarious Work' in Post-apartheid South Africa, 1994-2004," a doctoral dissertation submitted to York University, 2006.

making this 'elite' very precarious."[18] Nonetheless, differences in interests and practices between the "settled" proletariat and the more precariously employed – defined in terms of differential remuneration and job security and differing degrees of effective self-organization – can be of great relevance.[19]

It remains true, however, that COSATU has also retained an important role as an active and critical voice for both working-class and popular interests both within the Tripartite Alliance and more generally – and its present leader Zwelinzima Vavi continues as a spokesman of protest against what has happened on the ANC/SACP watch to any transformative hopes in South Africa.[20] At the same time, it is also the case that any potential that COSATU might hitherto have had to further develop itself, its goals and its possible vocation as a force for ongoing radical transformation through the mounting of some much more assertive counter-hegemonic alternative to capitalism, has, at least temporarily and with the rise to power of the ANC, been lost. As has any promise that the ANC might itself have seemed to offer as an organization capable of focussing working-class energies towards the realization of any such transformation.

3. The politics of the precariat: The civics and the UDF

And what of the precariat? In the following chapter (5) I will spell out the importance of this latter concept with reference to many settings of the Global South where an unfinished capitalist revolution continues to pile up populations in the global cities whose formal employment (if any) and

---

18   Eddie Webster, personal communication, although, as he correctly adds, "to have a job at all in these times may be seen as a privilege rather than a curse."

19   And so are differences between the "proletariat" and the urban "precariat" even more broadly defined – a distinction I will elaborate upon at the outset of the following section and in chapter 5, below.

20   Saul, "Liberating Liberation" (*op. cit.*)

whose life itself is generally and at best "precarious."[21] In such contexts, as I will further note, "the politics of the urban dwellers *per se* as distinct from that of the urban proletariat (there is some obvious overlap between categories of course) has a dynamic and thrust of its own." This is not just a matter of "street-level politics", although it is certainly that.[22] For what we see in such social circumstances, and alongside more specifically working-class action, is a "people" who are available for sociopolitical upsurge (in both township and rural settings) – though their actions may tend to be directed most forcefully against the state (especially at its local level) and the prevailing polity (as well as the latter's minions and programmes), than, directly, against the employers (and capitalism) *per se*.

In fact, it was just such a precariat, in its South African manifestation, that did set itself, in remarkable ways throughout the 1970s and 1980s, against the racial capitalist order, its rise to special prominence in the anti-apartheid resistance being first embodied by students, the sons and daughters of proletariat and precariat alike. Here, initially, the influence of "black consciousness" (BC) was front and centre – even if BC was always more a mood, "an idea whose time had come," than an organization. Far more a mood was to have particular resonance in sowing the seeds of what would become, so dramatically, "Soweto" – this latter term becoming crucial, both as fact and as symbol, to the dawning "South African revolution." For Soweto, in 1976, witnessed the outbreak of a student revolt destined to spread out from its point of origin and, over the next decade, to galvanize a broader resistance of historic magnitude throughout South Africa. As Bundy suggests, "between the Durban strikes of 1973 and the Mass Democratic Movement's defiance campaign of 1989, a long wave of popular protest surged across the South African political landscape. It

---

21   See my "What Working-Class?: Non-Transformative Global Capitalism and the African Case," in Baris Karagaac and Yasin Kaya, eds., *Capital and Labour in Contemporary Capitalism* (forthcoming), and chapter 5, below.

22   On this subject see, crucially, Jonathan Barker, *Street-Level Politics* (Toronto: Between the Lines, 1999).

eroded familiar landmarks and opened new channels, it lapped on the beachheads of white power, and its high tide left a residue of aspirations and expectations" of great significance.[23]

Not even the state's brutal repression could succeed in smothering the flames now so visible in so many centres throughout the country. Here in fact was a present-day expression, now dramatically magnified, of a long history of urban resistance to the closing fist of apartheid, a fightback cast both within the ANC tradition and outside it. Thus, in 1979-80, there was, as Bundy further records, "the shaping of a new tactical repertoire of grievance-based protests" and boycotts.[24] Moreover, this new kind of upsurge from below was to continue to trigger actions – actions to a very significant degree locally conceived and driven – that would erupt, throughout the 1980s, from an ever greater range of players and in an ever wider set of communities. True, although such varied initiatives were linked by their sharing of apartheid as the common denominator of mass oppression, these actions were not, by and large, centrally planned or coordinated. Nonetheless, the intensity of this new drive towards confrontation would mark a sea change in South Africa, etching the reality of a mass rejection of apartheid indelibly onto the perceptions of dominant classes, South Africa and global, but also of a global public more generally.

Of course, the state did make some move (as it had with Wiehann with respect to the proletariat) to respond to this new reality and to forestall trouble. Thus its Riekert Commission led to legislation that acceded to the stabilization, even legalization, of a black urban population's "rightful" presence in the cities – albeit in the terms of the familiar urban-rural split of the black population that had long underpinned racial capitalism. This

---

23 Colin Bundy, "Survival and Resistance: Township Organizations and Non-Violent Direct Action in Twentieth Century South Africa," in Glenn Adler and Jonny Steinberg, eds., *From Comrade to Citizen: The South African Civics Movement and the Transition to Democracy* (London and New York: Macmillan and St. Martin's Press, 2000), p. 26.

24 Bundy, "Survival and Resistance," p. 27.

was not nearly enough. But it did signal that the premises of the most lily-white of apartheid nostrums – under which blacks were conceived merely as "temporary sojourners" in the city – were themselves subject to change. And more moves of a similar nature were soon afoot: the "granting" of "Local Representative Councils" (albeit virtually toothless ones) to urban Africans, for example, and the attempt to oversee the incorporation of the country's Indian and Coloured communities as junior partners within a complex system of "own parliaments" for such groups. Almost immediately, however, any such "new constitutional dispensation" proved to be merely a further provocation, adding fuel to the mounting mood of resistance manifested by all segments of the "black" population (Africans, Indians and "Coloureds"). Indeed, it was this issue – the effective rejection, marked by massive non-participation within it, of the new governmental setup – that saw the birth of the UDF in August 1983.

The UDF, while not the motor of the myriad of local resistances that defined a proto-revolutionary moment in South Africa in the 1980s, and certainly not the sole voice to claim institutional preeminence (there were, after all, CUSA and other initiatives also in the lists), did become, to a significant degree, the presumptive *dirigeant* of South Africa's vast "precariat" in the townships – even though, as Popo Molefe, one time General-Secretary of the UDF, put it, the UDF was forever "trailing behind the masses."[25] Indeed, the UDF, with as many as 600 local affiliates at various points during the 1980s, became so central to resistance – perhaps the major agent in bringing South Africa, during the period 1984-86, as close to mass revolution as the country had ever been – that the state moved to smash it, banning it in 1988 and unleashing the full fury of police and military brutality on many of it leaders and functionaries.

True, the tension between the apparent petty-bourgeois ambitions of many of those who stepped forward to lead the UDF (and would become, in turn, recruits to the ANC phalanx that would step into public office with the organization's victory) on the one hand, and its more genuinely precarian "foot soldiers" who might have been persuaded by a different kind of leadership to keep the struggle for a more genuine liberation alive on the other, has often been commented upon. Yet the fact remains, as Seekings records, that a new high point was indeed reached with dramatic confrontations in 1984 in the Vaal Triangle and the East Rand "provoked by discontent over civic issues, especially increases in rents effected by unpopular township councilors, combined with student discontent around educational grievances and the state's constitutional reforms."[26] And after that, such resistance surged on: briefly stalled after 1986 by particularly savage state repression, including, as seen, a temporary banning of the UDF, it was, at the very end of the 1980s, resurgent again, its drive focussed by the Mass Democratic Movement, by COSATU and, finally, by a now unbanned and freshly defiant UDF.[27]

Yet the question remains: where did all this potential disappear to? Of course, to sustain any such revolutionary impulse as the UDF and the mass politics it embodied would have required imagination, a shift towards confronting a new enemy, poverty, in innovative and imaginative ways. But releasing active, assertive and sustained popular energies from below, and from an increasingly empowered citizenry, was the last thing a vanguardist, increasingly conservative, ANC actually was interested in – particularly as it became easier for the ANC to envisage itself soon coming to power. As many UDF leaders had begun to envisage a new order (and the new jobs that might go with it) the ANC itself moved to encourage the UDF, its task now, ostensibly, over, to formally dissolve itself.[28] As for the

26 Jeremy Seekings, "The Development of Strategic Thought in South Africa's Civic Movements, 1977-1990," in Adler and Steinberg, *From Comrade to Citizen*, p. 70.

27 This widespread campaign of naked suppression was a particularly important focus of the post-apartheid Truth and Reconciliation Commission.

28 Thus, Seekings, for one, can write in his book merely that, "less dramatically, the UDF faded away before finally disbanding formally in August, 1991. There was a

precariat, any future political role for it was to be relegated merely to the relative political passivity of voters' box participation, to the demobilized world of the newly created South African National Civic Organization and its wards amongst the "civics," and, in the absence of any more positively empowering vision, to such perverted popular purposes as would be evidenced in the xenophobic riots of 2008.[29]

For the fact is that the demise of the UDF marked a crucial moment in South Africa's recent history, albeit a moment too seldom given the careful scrutiny it warrants. Van Kessel notes, for example, the very tangible "demobilizing effect" of such a decision, with the ANC doing little or nothing, in the longer run, to sustain people's waning spirit of active militancy. She also quotes Alan Boesak as making a sharp distinction "between the UDF years and the early 1990s":

> He noted a widespread nostalgia for the UDF years. "That was a period of mass involvement, a period when people took a clear stand. That had a moral appeal. Now it is difficult to get used to compromises...Many people in the Western Cape now say that "the morality in politics has gone." The 1980s, that was "clean politics," morally upright, no compromises, with a clear goal."[30]

Similarly, Mona Younis reminds us that "as news of accommodation and concessions [during the 1990-94 period] to the previous rulers made their

---

certain inevitability to the organizational shift from the UDF to the ANC. ...[it was] a logical, unavoidable, even unremarkable event." Here, too, he quotes the then president of the South African Youth Congress, Peter Mokoba's 1991 statement: "Now that the ANC can operate legally, the UDF is redundant."

29   An option the weaknesses of which are crisply parsed by Seekings and by Elke Zoern in her *The Politics of Necessity: Community Organizing and Democracy in South Africa* (Madison: University of Wisconsin Press, 2011).

30   Ineke van Kessel, *'Beyond Our Wildest Dreams': The United Democratic Front and the Transformation of South Africa* (Charlottesville: The University Press of Virginia, 2000); see also Van Kessel's 'Trajectories after Liberation in South Africa: mission accomplished or vision betrayed?', in *Zuid-Afrika & Leiden* (University of Leiden, 2011, available at http://zuidafrikaleiden.nl).

way to the streets, union and community leaders and activists called for the reactivation of mass action."[31]

Indeed, as Younis continues, many had viewed the ANC's much talked-of "national democratic" stage as primarily to be thought of as a "transitional one toward the attainment of socialism." Small wonder that when the conference was convened to consider the possible dissolution of the UDF, it actually saw a clear and strong voicing of the view that, as an effective organ of "people's power," the UDF should be retained. "Proponents of this view," she writes, "envisaged the UDF's role as one of watching over the government, remaining prepared to activate mass action if the need should arrive. Many leaders and activists emphasized that the preservation of the UDF was imperative to ensure that participatory, rather than merely representative, democracy prevailed in South Africa." Of course, as we have seen, a majority at that conference ultimately sanctioned the disbanding of the UDF. Nonetheless, the loss of purpose this represented was a very damaging one.[32]

Or so, finally, Rusty Bernstein, the veteran and highly respected ANC and SACP member and militant, has testified most forcefully. Writing in the last year of his life (2000) Bernstein eloquently reflected on just why the liberation project to which he had devoted his life had become so unglued during the transition:

> Mass popular resistance revived again inside the country led by the UDF, [but] it led the ANC to see the UDF as an undesirable factor in the struggle for power and to undermine it as a rival focus for mass mobilization. It has undermined the

---

31 Mona Younis, *Liberation and Democratization: The South African and Palestinian National Movements* (Minneapolis: The University of Minnesota Press, 2000), p. 173.

32 Michelle Williams's valuable *The Roots of Participatory Democracy: Democratic Communists in South Africa and Kerala, India* (New York and London: Palgrave Macmillan, 2008), contrasts sharply the politics of Kerala's communist party with that of the ANC/SACP, emphasizing the latters' reliance on mere "mass mobilizing" – designed primarily to, in effect, draw a crowd to popularly hail its ascendancy. There could be very little place for a proactive UDF-like organization within such a scenario.

> ANC's adherence to the path [of] mass resistance as the way to liberation, and sub-
> stituted instead a reliance on manipulation of administrative power...It has impov-
> erished the soil in which ideas leaning towards socialist solutions once flourished
> and allowed the weed of "free market" ideology to take hold.[33]

From such a perspective, in short, it seems that the dissolution of the
UDF was rather less "logical," "unavoidable" and "unremarkable" than
Seekings (as cited in footnote 28, above) has claimed. For the ANC had
actually to work quite hard to see the UDF into its grave, quite literally
killing it off not for what it had done but for what, under another kind of
national leadership than the ANC was prepared to offer, the UDF initiative might have become.

This is not to deny the "continued radical instincts of [various] high-
quality unions, community-based organizations, women's and youth groups,
Non-Governmental Organizations, think-tanks, networks of CBOs and
NGOs, progressive churches, political groups and independent leftists."[34]
Indeed, all of these assertions – still manifest because of COSATU's survival
and despite the UDF's demise – were crucial to what Bond terms to have
been a "1994-96 surge of shopfloor, student and community wildcat protests."
True, the wave of such outbursts of popular discontent, mounted in the very
teeth of the deal between the ANC and capital, would temporarily subside.
Nonetheless, as Bond continues, they provided a meaningful bridge to the
awakened popular revolt that has since come to mark the new century – not
least, in this respect, the "IMF Riots [that] continued to break out in dozens
of impoverished black townships subject to high increases in service charges
and power/water cutoffs." Here, as we will emphasize in our conclusion to

---

33   In a letter to the present author, which, however, I subsequently published under
the title "Rusty Bernstein: A Letter." in *Transformation* (South Africa), No. 64,
2007.

34   Patrick Bond, *Elite Transition: From Apartheid to Neoliberalism in South Africa*
(London: Pluto Press, 2000), p. 168. On the rise (notably during the period of con-
stitutional negotiations) and fall of meaningful gender assertions, for example, see
Shireen Hassim, *Women's Organizations and Democracy in South Africa: Contesting
Authority* (Madison: University of Wisconsin Press, 2006).

this chapter, the promise of ongoing radical action by proletariat and precariat alike – a promise that Bernstein saw to lie, in part, at the base of the UDF – would continue to live.[35]

4. The ANC: The politics of the "possible"

Just who then was the slayer of revolutionary promise? We have implied an answer above, but here must underscore it. Thus John Daniel, in a sobering article entitled "Lusaka Wins," emphasizes not just the act of killing the UDF but also that of killing the latter's fundamental spirit. For the UDF, however much he may define it as being, in essence, "the ANC in disguise," is nonetheless seen to have been "a very different creature from its external progenitor": "in orchestrating a national insurrection" it was "not a centralized entity at all" but instead "one that practiced a robust and raucous form of participatory democracy in which a premium was placed on grassroots consensus and accountability. It was in most respects the antithesis of the essentially conformist ANC in exile."[36] Indeed, it was precisely this openness that the external wing of the ANC feared most, the possibility that the UDF would begin "to carry its practices into the emerging domestic structures of the ANC" – and even set in train a process of further radicalization. In sum, "hidden largely from the view of the so-called 'magic' of the Mandela era with its policies of rainbowism and reconciliation [and recolonization], a subterranean struggle for the heart and soul of the ANC ensued through the early and mid-1990s," a

---

35   See especially Ashwin Desai, *We are the Poors: Community Struggles in Post-Apartheid South Africa* (New York: Monthly Review Press, 2002); see also Peter Alexander, "Rebellion of the Poor: South Africa's Service Delivery Protests – a Preliminary Analysis," *Review of African Political Economy*, 37(123), 2010; and his updated survey entitled, "SA protest rates increasingly competitive with world leader China," 23 March 2012, available at http://www.amandlapublishers.co.za.

36   See John Daniel, "The Mbeki Presidency: Lusaka Wins," *South African Yearbook of International Affairs, 2001-02*, Johannesburg: South African Institute of International Affairs, 2002, pp. 7–15, from which I quote liberally in the next several paragraphs.

struggle capped by a victory for "Lusaka" with all its attendant negative implications.

In fact, Daniel goes further, rooting the "victory" in the much longer history of the ANC, insisting that the ANC was never a mass-based party ("it embraced notions of democracy, [but] was not popularly democratic in practice...In reality, it was a small, elite-led, top-down hierarchical party with neither a significant working class nor a rural base"). Indeed, it was this "*modus operandi*" that the ANC took into exile "where, in an initially hostile Western environment, in conditions of semi-clandestinity and heavily reliant on its Soviet and East German allies, it transmogrified into a tightly-knit, highly centralized vanguard party" – its political practice that of particularly strict democratic centralism, "with policy largely devised behind closed doors and then passed down to the lower ranks ... [and] deviation was met with expulsion and relegation."[37]

It therefore followed, ineluctably, that when the very top leadership of such an organization took, unequivocally, the capitalist road and used its newly-won power to consolidate such a choice it was "game over" for any who harboured, within the movement, some more radically democratic and/or socialist goals than those now enunciated by the vanguard. As McKinley writes, "many cadres in the movement [were] angered by the apparent abandonment of long held principles and policies." And yet, as he continues,

> the sheer pace with which the ANC leadership was traveling down the road of accommodation and negotiation instilled in its constituency the feeling there was no real alternative to a negotiated settlement which would entail compromise. This was further catalysed by the delegitimization of socialist polices (associated with the collapsed economies of the USSR and Eastern Europe) and the accompanying confusion and demoralization experienced by movement socialists.[38]

---

37   Daniel, 'The Mbeki Presidency,' pp. 9–10.

38   Dale McKinley, *The ANC and the Liberation Struggle: A Critical Political Biography* (London and Chicago: Pluto Press, 1997), p. 109.

Of course, it is precisely this that explains Bernstein's dismay when the opening offered by the UDF, with the radical possibilities that it revealed, were merely squandered by the ANC's top brass.

In addition to the overbearing influence on the ANC of the authoritarian ethos characteristic of the Soviet model, there was the quite similar ethos within both the front-line states bordering the region and the other liberation movements within the region itself with whom the ANC interacted.[39] For the war for southern African liberation was not a context that nurtured democracy in practice – even if its essential long-term goals were often presented in terms of democratic demands. Organizing for military confrontation against an absolutely unscrupulous and proactive enemy tended everywhere to privilege hierarchy, secrecy and even abuse of power on the part of those who would seek to lead any such resistance. Habits so formed would prove to be extremely difficult to shake.

Granted, such vanguardist militarism as marked the ANC did not lead readily to great success in terms of effective combat. In fact, from the Wankie campaign (an ill-starred military incursion into then Rhodesia, undertaken alongside Zimbabwean combatants, in 1967) forward, the ANC's practice of "guerilla struggle" did little, in and of itself, to shake the confidence of the regime. On the other hand, the drama of such sorties as the SASOL attacks in the early 1980s had a marked impact on growing popular self-confidence – as did Frelimo's defeat of the Portuguese in Mozambique in the 1970s and the Cuban/Angolan success against the South African Defence Force (SADF) at Cuito Cuanavale in the 1980s. At the same time, the real drama of the time was being played out inside the country, on the shop floors and in the townships themselves, in "rising social militancy and township unrest," as Elisabeth Drew emphasizes.[40]

---

39 See my "Socialism and Southern Africa," *op. cit.*

40 Elisabeth Jean Drew, *Forging Democracy from Below: Insurgent Transitions in South Africa and El Salvador* (Cambridge and New York: Cambridge University Press, 2000); see also Younis, *Liberation and Democratization*.

Why then were people so eager to accept the "jailed and exiled leadership of the ANC as [their] counter elite?," Drew asks, concluding that "the long-standing legitimacy of the ANC as opposition organization appears to have been part of the 'social memory of the opposition'" with, in addition, "the personal prestige of Nelson Mandela's leadership...unmatched by any other opposition figure." Similarly, Raymond Suttner, while arguing the case that there was, in fact, a more active ANC underground inside South Africa itself than many commentators have conceded, also admits that

> it was not inevitable or preordained that the ANC would achieve hegemony within the liberation struggle and the new democratic South Africa. Indeed, there were times in the history of the organization when it was virtually dormant...

> That it did survive [however] depended in the first place on the way in which the ANC had, over decades, inserted itself into the cultural consciousness of people, becoming part of their sense of being, even if at times of great repression there was no public forum of outlet for this identity.[41]

Here, perhaps, is one crucial reason why the ANC established its hegemony within the anti-apartheid struggle – and, in the process, "got away," at least temporarily, with shrinking that struggle's overall thrust to one of "mere" nationalist assertion. For at this potent level of the popular imagination, the ANC/SACP/MK (Umkhonto weSizwe) tandem came to serve even more as forceful myth than as reality – this also being true of the quasi-mythological status that had accrued to Mandela while he was in prison during the 1980s. The result: when a capitalist-friendly ANC was beckoned, as Fanon had once said, to "settle the problem" around "the green baize table before any regrettable act has been performed or irreparable gesture made," the stage had also been set, within the

---

41 Raymond Suttner, *The ANC Underground in South Africa* (Aukland Park, S.A.: Jacana, 2008), p. 148. Indeed, in the words of one other incisive analysis (Kurt Schock, *Unarmed Insurrections: People's Power Movements in Nondemocracies* [Minneapolis: University of Minnesota Press, 2000, p. 66]), "more important to the anti-apartheid than the threat of armed insurrection" was "the ANC's reestablished public presence after the Soweto uprising and its provision of a culture of resistance and [of] popular anti-apartheid frames."

resistance movement more generally, for the ANC's eventual accession to formal power.[42]

It must therefore be underscored that the ANC's compromise reached with capital was no accident.[43] As early as 1984, future president Thabo Mbeki had written boldly and presciently that "the ANC is not a socialist party. It has never pretended to be one, it has never said it was, and it is not trying to be. It will not become one by decree or for the purpose of pleasing its 'left' critics."[44] Thus, in the late eighties, he and his cronies would seal a deal with capital on behalf of the ANC – adroitly outflanking Chris Hani and other potential critics within the movement as he did so.[45] Soon, too, even the sainted Mandela – despite his provocative statements about nationalizations and other aspects of economic strategy upon his release from prison in 1990 – would retreat from such heterodox thoughts. The ANC was well launched on its two-track process of negotiations – negotiations with both capital *and* the apartheid state – to determine the outcome of South Africa's struggle for liberation. Small wonder Hein Marais could conclude that, among other things, it was clear that by 1994 "the left had lost the macroeconomic battle."[46]

---

42 Frantz Fanon, *The Wretched of the Earth* (Harmondsworth: Penguin Books, 1967), p. 48; as he then continues, "if the masses, without waiting for the chairs to be arranged around the baize table, listen to their own voice and begin committing outrages and setting fire to buildings, the elites and the bourgeois parties will be seen running to the colonialists to exclaim 'this is very serious! We do not know how it will end; we must find a solution – some sort of compromise.'"

43 Neville Alexander, *An Ordinary Country: Issues in the Transition from Apartheid to Democracy in South Africa* (Pietermaritzburg: University of Natal Press, 2002).

44 Thabo Mbeki, "The Fatton Thesis: A Rejoinder," *Canadian Journal of African Studies*, 18(3), 1984, p. 609.

45 This "Hani moment" is graphically discussed in Janet Smith and Beauregard Trump, *Hani: A Life Too Short* (Johannesburg and Cape Town: Jonathan Ball Publishers, 2009). Hani's intervention at the NWC is referenced to Gevisser on p. 210.

46 Hein Marais, *South Africa – Limits to Change: The Political Economy of Transition* (London and Cape Town: Zed Press and University of Cape Town Press, 1998). A revised second edition of this valuable work appeared in 2001.

As for the broader movement, it had been pulled emotionally past any lingering black consciousness or "workerist" sensibility and, ever more firmly, onto the ANC's symbolic terrain. What might have happened had a political organization like the ANC sought to build on and to draw out the revolutionary possibilities of the time is now a matter of merely disempowered speculation. The hard fact remains that ANC leadership was, quite simply, prepared to reach a deal, defined largely on global and local capital's own terms, in order both to guarantee the consolidation of a colour-blind, formally democratic but capitalist-friendly, overall outcome and also to ensure its own coming to power.

5. Agents of deformed change I: Capital and the politics of possession

For much of the twentieth century the phrase "racial capitalism" accurately epitomized the nature of a social and economic system in South Africa that was intractable, even seemingly invulnerable. In this system the twin pillars of dominant social power in South Africa – the racist overrule that culminated in apartheid and the class rule inherent in capitalism's centrality to the country's economy – came to complement each other, with any possible contradictions between the two modes of ordering social hierarchy merely smoothed away with relative ease.

True, some have insisted in seeing these two hierarchical modes – that of racial domination and that of class differentiation – as being in stark contradiction (as indeed they might appear to be in the realm of abstract model-building). This could then be presented as, on the one hand, racial prejudice trumping profit while, on the other hand, a colour-blind capitalism being forced to concede costly and "uneconomic" ground to the captains of racial domination.[47] But this is quite misleading. As Frederick Johnstone has clearly demonstrated, a crucial "exploitation colour-bar"

---

47   The classic example of this argument is that of Merle Lipton in her *Capitalism and Apartheid* (Aldershot, U.K.: Gower Publishing, 1985), p. 372.

(favouring capital) was merely complemented by a "job colour bar" (favouring, up to a point, white workers). For Johnstone demonstrated that any tension between the demands for entitlement based on the claims of race and class is best understood as representing relatively mild jockeyings for advantage within an overall structure of shared white-skin-cum-capitalist-class privilege.[48]

It was this reality, of course, that led Biko in the 1970s to his conclusion that it was racial privilege that tied the entire South African system together – with "black consciousness" thus becoming the key ingredient in any meaningful radical endeavour in the country. Interestingly, however, it is also true that, even as Biko spoke, the grounds for such a stark premise were beginning to slip away. This was most evident, initially, within the camp of capital itself. To begin with, some fractions of capital felt themselves to be more constrained by apartheid than others, notably, in this respect, certain sectors of manufacturing capital that could sense the super-exploitation of blacks as defining a constraint on the wider domestic markets they sought. Moreover, as a more complex capitalism also emerged, the various racial discriminations within the job market – even though the apartheid system was often rather more flexible about them in practice than in theory – could also be felt as a constraint upon the capitalists' effective deployment of any and all labour, regardless of its pigment.

But the die was really cast when the unrest of the 1970s, already visible enough to unsettle both capital and the apartheid state, escalated, from 1984 on, into the broad-scale eruption of black action. In such a context, the defection of capitalists from the apartheid project (albeit initially and most markedly the English-speaking of them) escalated dramatically.[49]

---

48   See, crucially, Fredrick Johnstone, "White Prosperity and White Supremacy in South Africa Today," *African Affairs*, 69(April), 1970; and his *Class, Race, and Gold: A Study of Class Relations and Racial Discrimination in South Africa* (London: Routledge, 1976).

49   On such realities see Dan O'Meara's *Forty Lost Years: The Apartheid State and the*

For many now saw – as some had already seen in the 1970s – the dangers in continuing to link the exploitation (indeed super-exploitation) that they thrived upon any too tightly to the racial repression that marked the "racial capitalist" system. Indeed, with mass African resistance continuing to escalate in the 1980s, the oft-quoted remark of big-business insider Zac de Beer takes on its appropriate resonance: "We all understand how years of apartheid have caused many blacks to reject the economic as well as political system...We dare not allow the baby of free enterprise to be thrown out with the bathwater of apartheid."[50] Of even more significance, perhaps, was the 1985 comment by Gavin Relly, then Chairman of the powerful Anglo-American Corporation, who noted after the fateful meeting in Lusaka of leading capitalists with the ANC leadership that he had the impression that the ANC was not "too keen" to be seen as "marxist" and that he felt they had a good understanding "of the need for free enterprise."[51] Time was to demonstrate fully just how perceptive was Relly's 1985 reading of the ANC's own emerging mindset.

As Dan O'Meara reminds us, American and British capitalists were themselves beginning to rethink the odds in South Africa and to step back from apartheid.[52] Recall, in this connection, the dramatic conclusions of Malcolm Fraser, the deeply conservative former Australian Prime Minister, and a key member of the Commonwealth's official mission sent to South Africa in 1986 to evaluate the situation there. He was also author of the mission's eloquent and tough-minded report, one that called for an extension of sanctions against South Africa in order to force it to come to its senses before the confrontation there escalated out of control. As Fraser further warned, in an escalating conflict "moderation would be

---

Politics of the National Party, 1948-1994 (Randberg, S.A. and Athens, Ohio: Ravan Press and Ohio University Press, 1996).

50   As quoted in the *Financial Times*, 10 June 1986.

51   As cited in McKinley, *The ANC and the Liberation Struggle*, p. 109.

52   O'Meara, *op. cit.*, pp. 328–341 and *passim*.

On Taming a Revolution: The South African Case ∞ 87

swept aside...The government that emerged from all of this would be extremely radical, probably Marxist, and would nationalize all western business interests."[53] Fraser's warning would in turn inspire Brian Mulroney, Canada's Prime Minister to put sanctions on the Canadian political agenda but also to push for them both within the Commonwealth and in the G-7. Mulroney was not successful at first in the latter forum but then, slowly, Margaret Thatcher and, albeit with even greater reluctance, Ronald Reagan began to come over to such an understanding – all the more so as the global "threat" of the Soviet bloc itself appeared to wane.

To be sure, capital's new caution was also framed by the escalation of public pressure upon it from an emboldened anti-apartheid movement in the West – now responding dramatically to the unsettled economic horizon a turbulent South Africa had begun to present to the world.[54] But note, too, that a continuing and concerted effort to win over the ANC to a post-apartheid order extremely friendly to capitalism was clearly afoot – and beginning to promise results. Not that, in the event, much persuading of the ANC's exile group seemed to be required – even though it meant jettisoning the more elaborate dreams of a socialist future that many in the ANC/SACP had once professed to harbour.

6. Agents of deformed change II:
The apartheid state and the politics of postponed promise

While Afrikaner capitalists moved a bit more slowly towards such an understanding, something of a sea change had begun to occur even within the Afrikaner polity nonetheless. Thus, O'Meara and others have demonstrated clearly the manner in which the fault lines of class distinction within Afrikanerdom had begun to eat away at the *volk* – and at the

---

53   Malcolm Fraser, "No More Talk. Time to Act," *Times* (London), 30 June 1986.

54   On this, see my *A Partial Victory: The North American Campaign for Southern African Liberation in Global Perspective* (New York: Monthly Review Press, forthcoming).

National Party itself.[55] For the class character of "Afrikanerdom," the chief electoral base of the ruling National Party, was visibly shifting, however slowly and uncertainly, and the party itself had begun to fray.

In fact, difficult as it may now be to remember, P.W. Botha – even granted that he was ever the bully – came to prime-ministerial office, in the wake of Voster and Muldergate, as a reformer, a *verligte* over and against the serried ranks of *verkramptes*. Of course, he would seek to "reform" in order to preserve – to preserve, in his case, the racial hierarchy, rather than the much more unequivocal alternative of "mere" class hierarchy that the capitalists would increasingly offer as the eighties dragged on. Indeed, his successor, F.W. de Klerk, would prove ultimately to be of Botha's persuasion as well, although he would feel forced to go even further in a "reform" direction than had his presidential predecessor – while still, almost to the very end, trying to safeguard some attributes of the racist order itself.

Thus, in the 1970s and as a new wave of popular agitation begins to surface that was fired by both proletariat and precariat in the cities and in the townships, Botha and others sensed that some preemptive initiatives, beyond the Bantustan strategy and brute force, were also advisable.[56] As a result, and as part of a "Total Strategy" that Botha and coterie now favoured and advocated, several novel attempts, noted above, at "formative action" were undertaken – as framed, notably, by the Wiehann and Riekert reports. The results, as the renewed (and quite dramatic) internal uprising of the mid-1980s would soon show, were to be quite different from any mere domesticating of resistance, however. For the fact is that Botha, the Nats, and the apartheid state more generally, were now trying to do several seemingly contradictory things at the same time.

The problem followed from their very interpretation of "Total Strategy", of course – an interpretation that also rationalized the formidable

---

55   O'Meara's *Forty Lost Years* remains, as noted above, the *locus classicus* of analysis of the National Party's trajectory – from egg to earth as it were.

56   See again, on the distinction between "proletariat" and "precariat," my "What Working-Class?" (ch. 5, below).

centralization of power and command into Botha's own hands as Prime Minister (later President), and, under his leadership, into the hands of the "securocrats" of the police and (especially) the military.[57] Professing themselves to be following the lead of such global gurus as Beaufre and Huntington, this "security state" sought to "reform" and to "liberalize" just enough to take the steam out of the kettle of popular protest – but to make such (limited) "reform" stick with as much force as would prove to be "necessary."

In doing so – the acceptance of black trade unions, for example, and the legalizing of the permanency of the presence of some significant numbers of blacks in the urban areas – the Nats did, to be sure, move some distance away from the main premises of traditional "apartheid." Far enough at any rate to accelerate the rightward drift of many amongst the lower ranks of Afrikanerdom who felt themselves to be threatened by change and who now came to strengthen the ranks of Andres Treuernicht's Conservative Party, and other such dark forces of genuine reaction as Eugene Terreblanche and his Afrikaner Weerstandsbeweging (AWB) and Constand Viljoen and his Freedom Front.

Nonetheless the "reform" so envisaged could actually do very little to quell the popular (black) rejection of the fundamentally racist predilections of Nat reformers. For the black population increasingly sought not some mildly improved terms within the overall apartheid framework of power but, instead, a full-scale change, democratic and transformative, of that very framework; it was on this basis that the push from below that fired the popular uprising of 1984-86 was launched in fact. Of course, this is also precisely where the other, darker side of Total Strategy came so grimly into play. For the policing function of the "security state" was now deemed to be absolutely essential. And, finely honed as such a state apparatus had been through the preceding decades of imposing apartheid,

57   See Philip Frankel, *Pretoria's Praetorians: Civil Military Relations in South Africa* (Cambridge: Cambridge University Press, 1984).

it was fully prepared to be tough, brutal and merciless enough to attempt to force the African population to be (rather less than) "half-free" – and to keep quiet about the rest.

This remorseless side of the story cannot be rehearsed here. Suffice to say that there was now locked into place a reign of terror by the state, the abuse of power that this embodied providing much of the focus for the post-apartheid Truth and Reconciliation Commission. True, such a preoccupation would come, negatively, to deflect the TRC's attention away from the more mundane structures of corporate and political power that had long sanctioned and bolstered apartheid. Nonetheless, there were more than enough chilling accounts of the impact of this underside of Bothaism presented to serve as a useful reminder of just what apartheid had actually meant in practice over all the years of its grim sway.[58]

Meanwhile, the neoliberal clock was ticking for the Nats as well. Indeed, the latter-day economic strategy of the National Party-in-power was itself, by the end of the 1980s, increasingly premised on the freshly established neoliberal script being written by global capitalism. This was why, despite Botha's bluster, so many even within the apartheid government were particularly alert to negative signals from that quarter, and why the South African state now sought to create an ever more free market context within which capital could operate quite freely. Of course, this might appear to be somewhat counterintuitive in light of Botha's own otherwise *dirigiste*, and still quite racist, approach to the overall society. But it was precisely onto this kind of economic terrain that capital, and an increasing number of centrist political actors, sought, with ultimate success, to draw in the ANC – itself, in any case, an increasingly willing "victim" of this particular ploy.

In the event de Klerk himself advanced this "strategy" dramatically, although, like Botha, he did not yield up any such "reform" entirely

---

58   See, among others, the six volume official report of the TRC (Cape Town: Truth and Reconciliation Commission, 1998); as well as numerous nightmarish book length accounts of the period.

straightforwardly. For he too was still trying to have it both ways. Thus, after his release of Mandela and unbanning of the ANC, he continued, throughout most of the subsequent transition period, to deploy the state's cruel apparatus of enforcement, manifesting (to put it charitably) a toleration of the malign activities of various so-called "third force" elements and of Mangosuthu Buthelezi's bloodthirsty cohort in an attempt to either defeat the ANC outright or, if not that, at least to skew the transition in the direction of more white-friendly outcomes. Not for de Klerk, until very late in the day, any mere reliance on shared trans-racial class interests to safeguard privilege beyond apartheid. Nonetheless, in the end and after a bumpy road (the grim events of Bisho and Boipatong massacres and the killing fields of KwaZulu and the Vaal townships demonstrating the abyss that threatened to swallow the country) de Klerk came to feel he had no choice. Between chaos and the acceptance of a new ruling-class coalition transcending race he saw, ultimately, no realistic, more overtly racist, choice.

7. A disfigured transition

With capital, local and global, increasingly on side, and the proletariat and precariat more or less brought to heel (now both to be rendered politically as presumptive "citizens" rather than as active comrades in a continuing struggle for genuine liberation) the stage was set for transition – or was it? For there were a number of other bridges to be crossed during the four deeply troubled years that separated Mandela's release in 1990 and the unbanning of the ANC and the SACP from the first genuinely free, all-in, election of 1994 – and there were a number of other players at the transition table to be dealt with cautiously, even somewhat nervously.

To begin with, in the prevailing context of quasi-stalemate, there was the substantial residue of an apartheid polity, state and army, still holding the reins of governmental power with none of these quite certain as to how much political power they could or should concede. In this crucial sphere alone the spectres of "power-sharing," ethnic vetoes and much worse could be seen to loom. There was also Gatsha Buthelezi, the Zulu leader, never quite a "stooge" of the government but someone who was quite prepared to become its active partner in countering, in blood, the ANC. There was the white right, too, from Eugene Terreblanche and his AWB (though this force would eventually disqualify itself with its ill-fated raid into Bophutatswana) through to General Viljoen. The latter's own vaunted presence was, in fact, ultimately to dwindle away into an unsuccessful bid for a special volkstaat to be created for exclusive Afrikaner presence within the broader boundaries of South Africa, but not before his movement, the Freedom Front, posed a shadowy threat, like that from Buthelezi, right up until a few days before the election. In the end, however, the ANC did win – although capital did too.

How then accurately to interpret all this?

For starters, we are here carried back to our initial paragraphs on Biko and Fanon. After all, Fanon was the most scorching critic of the false decolonization that Biko thought South Africa might, because of its distorted, racially-structured nature, be spared. But recall Fanon's classic shorthand description (which we repeat again in chapter 6, below) of decolonization in the more northern parts of Africa where independence had arrived while he was still alive:

> The national middle class discovers its historic mission: that of intermediary. Seen through its eyes, its mission has nothing to do with transforming the nation; it consists, prosaically, of being the transmission line between the nation and a capitalism, rampant though camouflaged, which today puts on the masque of neo-colonialism [recolonization].[59]

Isn't this what we can see all too clearly to have happened in South Africa as well: a power-grab by a middle class risen from among the recently oppressed population who now, riding the back of "liberation," had thrust

---

59   Fanon, *Wretched of the Earth*, p. 122. As Fanon continues, "The national middle class will be quite content with the role of the Western bourgeoisie's business agent and it will play the part without any complexes in a most dignified manner."

themselves forward, both in the state and the private sector, to take the role of well rewarded junior partners of global capital?

There are, of course, other perspectives. Some will merely offer the self-exculpatory argument that "globalization made me do it" as sufficient explanation of the ANC's capitulation to capitalism: the Soviet bloc quickly disappearing, a much too powerful capitalist system, global and domestic, left standing. This is the kind of "fatalism" offered up by many ANC apologists: mere resignation to "necessity" as the rationale for the government's opting quite unapologetically for capitalism. True, such capitulation is often presented as being social-democratically tinged, but the essence of the position is clear: Africa and Africans have no choice; whatever the outcome of taking the present tack, "there is no alternative." Small wonder that South African President Thabo Mbeki could himself, famously and quite specifically, state (and with some apparent glee), "just call me a Thatcherite."[60]

No less an observer than Naomi Klein (in her *Shock Doctrine*) has argued, however, a different view, seeing the ANC instead as prisoners of capital – however short-sighted and naïve they may have been with regard to the dangers of any such entanglements. Klein, in fact, calls up some strong witnesses to support her view: South African economist Vishnu Padayachee, for example, whom she paraphrases as arguing that "none of this happened because of some grand betrayal on the part of the ANC leaders but simply because they were outmaneuvered on a series of issues that seemed less than crucial at the time – but turned out to hold South Africa's lasting liberation in the balance." Similarly, William Gumede's view, as directly quoted, is that

> "if people felt [the political negotiations] weren't going well there would be mass protests. But when the economic negotiators would report back, people thought it was technical." This perception was encouraged by Mbeki, who portrayed the talks

---

60 Thabo Mbeki, as cited in William Gumede, *Thabo Mbeki and the Battle for the Soul of the ANC* (Cape Town: Zebra Press, 2005), p. 89, in speaking at the June 1996 launching of the GEAR programme.

as "administrative" and as being of no popular concern. As a result he [Gumede] told me, with great exasperation, "We missed it! We missed the real story."

Gumede, Klein further notes, "came to understand that it was at those "technical" meetings that the true future of his country was being decided – though few understood it at the time." But, one is tempted to ask, had Padayachee and Gumede not read their Fanon? For Klein's own position is, like theirs, fundamentally incorrect.[61] It is impossible, in fact, to imagine that the ANC leadership, having sought assiduously from at least the mid-1980s to realize just such an outcome, such a false decolonization, could simply have "missed it" – missed, that is, the main point of what was happening to South Africa.

Hence the decision, by the now powerful, merely to instead celebrate capitalism, its present and its ostensibly promising future. One might think this is a difficult position for any concerned African to take in light of recent history. Yet in elevated circles in South Africa it has become simply commonsense. Mandela, for one and despite having an apparently alternative vision immediately on his release from prison, came to embrace a firmly capitalist South Africa in just such a "commonsensical" manner.[62] And Trevor Manuel, Tito Mboweni, Thabo Mbeki and others have too – with many other erstwhile ANC activists also moving briskly into the private sector.[63] Moreover, as further evidence to support such an interpretation, Patrick Bond has itemized a whole set of highly ques-

---

61 Vishnu Padayachee and William Gumede as quoted in Naomi Klein, *The Shock Doctrine: The Rise of Disaster Capitalism* (Toronto: Alfred A. Knopf Canada, 2007), chapter 10, "Democracy Born in Chains: South Africa's Constricted Freedom," pp. 233–261.

62 Recall his apparent hailing, in 1994, of the free market as a "magic elixir" in his speech to the joint session of the Houses of Congress in Washington.

63 Indeed, some of these latter were also to be involved in the breakaway COPE movement that, in the wake of Mbeki's overthrow and in a (hostile but largely mistaken) anticipation of Zuma's radicalization of the ANC project, launched itself in 2008 – and contested the 2009 election, not very successfully, as a possible national liberation-linked alternative to the right of the ANC.

tionable but crucial economic policy choices friendly to global capital made during the first half-decade of ANC power, from "agreeing to pay illegitimate apartheid era debt in part by taking on an unnecessary IMF loan of US\$750 million (1993) with predictable strings attached" to "adopting a bound-to-fail neoliberal economic policy and insulating the Reserve Bank from democracy so as to raise interest rates to South Africa's highest real levels ever."[64] Indeed, by 1996, the ANC leadership had crafted for itself and the country the firmly neoliberal GEAR ("Growth, Employment and Reconstruction") strategy – declared by Trevor Manuel, to be "non-negotiable" – to replace 1994's mildly more left-leaning RDP ("Reconstruction and Development Programme").[65]

Interestingly, Pippa Green's hagiographical biography of Manuel, one of the chief architects of the ANC's economic strategy, is entitled, boldly and altogether instructively, *Choice, Not Fate*.[66] In its pages we find the case for recolonization being presented as, primarily, a smart developmental choice.[67] Similarly, Alan Hirsch, from his vaunted position as "Chief Director of Economic Policy at the Presidency, South Africa," has averred that "the intellectual paradigm within which the ANC operates" is one in which "elements of a northern European approach to social development [are] combined with elements of Asian approaches within conservative

---

64   Patrick Bond, "South African Splinters: From 'Elite Transition' to 'Small-a Alliances.'" *Review of African Political Economy*, No. 127(March), 2001, p. 115. On this subject there is also Patrick Bond's *Elite Transition* (*op. cit.*); for another very full picture of the increasingly narrowing limits placed by ANC on its economic policy-making see Marais, *South Africa*.

65   On the RDP see my exchange with Bill Freund, "The RDP: Two Reviews," *Southern Africa Report*, July, 1994.

66   Pippa Green, *Choice, Not Fate: The Life and Times of Trevor Manuel* (Rosebank, S.A.: Penguin Books, 2008). The book itself is a startling example of hagiography (both as regards Manuel and also the ANC at its most conservative) but the lead title is also an arresting shorthand advertisement for the way in which the ANC would apparently like to present itself to right-thinking readers.

67   We might be forgiven for thinking to be not quite so "smart" from the point of view of the vast mass of the South African population, of course.

macroeconomic parameters."[68] Some beneficiaries of this choice will have had quite self-interested and crass motives for making it, of course. Others (Hirsch perhaps) may have thought – this being the perennial illusion of social democrats everywhere – that you can "permit" capital to do the heavy lifting of accumulation and the provisioning of material requirements while "the good guys," from on high, and through taxation and a variety of not too onerous "controls," bend such a capitalist system to meet a range of humane social preferences and less tangibly material "needs."

Lost in this latter project, however, is the way in which class imperatives and the uneven distribution of power almost inevitably rot out shared social purpose under capitalism – even as capitalism is also fostering a culture of consumerism and "possessive individualism" unlikely to sustain any alternative, more high-minded, politics. Operating here is a kind of Gresham's law that affects mildly progressive politics, under which "law" one witnesses the gradual debasing of the coinage of progressive sociopolitical purpose and instead the fostering of a merely parasitic state and a self-seeking governing class. This is, at best, what I would myself judge to have become of South Africa's presumed transition – and even this kind of pretense as to the retention of some higher aspiration and some higher purpose is fast fading in ruling circles.

*　*　*

Still, it ain't over 'til it's over. Indeed, South Africa is currently very close to being the world's leader in grassroots social protest and demonstrated dissidence. True, as I have observed elsewhere, this unrest, this "rebellion of the poor" (in Peter Alexander's evocative phrase), remains more locally focussed (as protest) than nationally focussed – not yet being integrally linked to some presumptive counter-hegemonic project that might effectively challenge the ANC and its project while also aiming at

---

68   Alan Hirsch, *Season of Hope: Economic Reform Under Mbeki and Mandela* (Pietermaritzburg: University of Kwazulu-Natal Press, 2005), p. 4.

a much more genuine liberation than the country has as yet come even close to realizing. Yet the voices of dissent are many and their potential real.[69] Indeed, there are even signs that, "fuelled by a dangerous mixture of high unemployment, slow growth, weak leadership and fierce feuding within the governing party," some "influential factions" in the ANC itself are "pushing to transform the courts, the media, the economy and...the much praised constitution."[70] Can one not see in this diverse contestation, both within and without the ANC, the slow dawning of the "next liberation struggle," a continuation of the very popular struggle that, as we have seen in this essay, the ANC leadership – in the name of neoliberalism and what one can only call "recolonization" – had worked so hard to thwart in the transition years from the mid-1980s to the mid-1990s?

---

69   See my "Liberating Liberation" (*op. cit.*); and also Alexander, "Rebellion of the Poor" as well as his "SA protest rates."

70   Geoffrey York, "ANC's radical voices growing louder: Proposed agenda includes black economic ownership, farm expropriation, nationalization and tighter controls on the courts," *The Globe and Mail* (Toronto), 8 June 2012.

CHAPTER 5

The New Terms of Resistance
Proletariat, Precariat and the Present African Prospect[1]

Everywhere the logic of an ever more globalized capitalist economy has shifted the global goal posts – as regards both the nature of on-going capitalist exploitation and of resistance to it. For starters we must face centrally the fact that global capitalism, even if still profoundly controlling of the world economy, no longer has the promise to transform the world in any entirely straightforward manner: to, that is, vastly simplify its social contradictions as it once promised/threatened to do. As Marx and Engels, for example, once thought it would:

> Our epoch, the epoch of the bourgeiosie, possesses...its distinctive feature: it has simplified the class antagonisms. Society as a whole is more and more splitting into two great hostile camps, into two great classes directly facing each other: Bourgeoisie and Proletariat...The bourgeoisie has stripped of its halo every occupation hitherto honoured and looked at with reverent awe. It has converted the physician, the lawyer, the priest, the poet, the man of science, into its paid wage-labourers... The other classes decay and finally disappear in the face of Modern Industry; the proletariat is its special and essential product.[2]

---

1   This essay, originally prepared for a workshop organized by David Harvey at CUNY in New York, May 2011, first appeared, in a rather different form, in Baris Karagaac and Yasin Kaya (eds.), *Capital and Labour in Contemporary Capitalism* (forthcoming).

2   Karl Marx and Friedrich Engels, "Manifesto of the Communist Party" in Robert C.

Instead, in much of the Global South (and perhaps particularly in Africa, the region of the world that is of my particular interest) the transformation is, as best, incomplete. Global capitalism has certainly become a dominant reality, one quite capable of imposing upon Africa, for example, a grid of continuing inequality, exploitation and the recolonization of ostensibly liberated and independent peoples in the interests of corporate profit. Yet the system now in place is quite incapable of producing anything like the relatively straightforward, and theoretically bi-polar and proto-revolutionary, society of bourgeoisie and proletariat, either now or in any foreseeable future. In fact, much of the Global South is, quite simply, trapped between history's ostensible phases in ways that we shall have to examine below. Undoubtedly a key feature of this change is the ever-increasing saliency of what has come to be termed "precarious work." We will have to explore this reality. But we will also have to examine the even more basic and more general reality of "precarious populations" existing more generally throughout the South – not least those who embody in their persons the phenomenal growth of the urban areas in Africa (as elsewhere in the Global South), our principal focus. What implications must this have for our time-honoured sense of the "working class" as epitomized in its most organized and its most generic essentials – and also of our attendant sense of the "revolutionary agency" that the "working class" has, on the left, typically been thought uniquely to exemplify? How best now – in the world of both proletariat *and* precariat – to articulate the possible terms of any effective challenge from below to the inhuman, inequitable and exploitative capitalist system that continues to dominate Africa (and not least South Africa, my own focus)

Tucker (ed.), *The Marx-Engels Reader*, Second Edition (New York: W. W. Norton, 1978), pp. 474, 476, 482. At the same time, of course, they write (p. 481) that "the organization of the proletarians into a class, and consequently into a political party, is continually being upset by competition between the workers themselves," – adding, however, that "it [the proletariat] ever rises again, stronger, firmer, mightier."

and to produce as many unsavoury outcomes as it does? If not merely a "proletarian revolution," what then?

I. Precarious Work in Africa and Beyond: The Ambiguities of the "Working Class"

Here we will let the fashionable *Wikipedia* – because in its relevant entry it draws so heavily on the estimable scholarly work of Fudge, Owens and Vosko – give us a first lead on our topic, precisely with regard to "precarious work":

> Precarious work is a term used to describe non-standard employment which is poorly paid, insecure, unprotected and cannot support a household. In recent decades there has been a dramatic increase in precarious work due to such factors as: globalization, the shift from the manufacturing sector to the service sector, and the spread of information technology. These changes have created a new economy which demands flexibility in the workplace and, as a result, caused the decline of the standard employment relationship and a dramatic increase in precarious work. An important aspect of precarious work is its gendered nature, as women are continuously over-represented in this type of work. Precarious work is frequently associated with the following types of employment: "part-time employment, self-employment, fixed-term work, temporary work, on-call work, homeworkers and telecommuting." All these forms of employment are related in that they depart from the standard employment relationship (full-time, continuous employment with one employer). Each form of precarious work may offer its own challenges but they all share the same disadvantages: low wages, few benefits, lack of collective representation, and little to no job security.[3]

Moreover, in Africa such a definition/ description actually begins to describe the vast bulk of the urban population, so great in their numbers that, as many more flock into the urban areas, they are hard-pressed to find any formal "work" at all, even of the kind most readily defined as being "precarious" – not so much "precarious workers," then, as they

---

3   This Wikipedia entry draws heavily on Judy Fudge and Rosemary Owens (eds.), *Precarious Work, Women and the New Economy: The Challenge to Legal Norms* (Toronto: Hart, 2006), especially their introduction, and also on Leah Vosko's chapter in the same book, "Gender, Precarious Work and the International Labour Code: The Ghost in the ILO Closet."

are, as noted above, "precarious populations." And it is here that the most orthodox Marxist may be tempted to throw up his/her hands in despair, faced with the reality of an emergent "capitalist" society very different from the kind – one much more straightforward, at least in theory, in terms of revolutionary potential – that Marx and Engels had foreseen (as quoted in our opening paragraph) to be slowly but surely simplifying and clarifying social contradictions. Should we be surprised that some Marxists are in fact tempted to view with such alarm the kind of society that a powerful but nonetheless non-transformative (or, at the very least, not as yet transformative) capitalism does produce in Africa and elsewhere in many parts of the Global South? For, to repeat, such "intermediate" (and not necessarily "transitional"!) societies seem – in Africa certainly – very unlikely to alter substantially into some entirely straightforward and conventionally "bourgeoisie-proletariat" pattern of polarization in the near future.

Of course, Marx and Engels themselves spoke nervously of the social realities they saw to be scarring the transitional period to a full-bodied capitalism, noting, in particular, the possible resonance of a resultant (in their term) "dangerous class," one defined by them as

> the social scum, that passively rotting mass thrown up by the lowest layers of the old society, [which] may, here and there, be swept into the movement by a proletarian revolution; its conditions of life, however, prepare it far more for the part of a bribed tool of reactionary intrigue.[4]

As Marx himself writes elsewhere, "Alongside decayed roués with dubious means of subsistence and dubious origins, alongside ruined and reckless casts of the bourgeoisie, were vagabonds, discharged soldiers, discharged jailbirds, escaped gallery-slaves, swindlers, mountebanks, *lazzeroni*, pickpockets, tricksters, gamblers, *maquereaus* [procurers], brothel-keepers, porters, *literati* [literary hacks] organ-grinders, rag-pickers, knife-grinders, tinkers, beggars – in short the whole indefinite,

---

4   Marx and Engels, *ibid.*, p. 482.

disintegrated mass, thrown hither and thither, which the French term *la bohemia*."[5] In addition, in a second and related text, he speaks critically of the Mobile Guards, the most assertive strike force mobilized on behalf of France's reactionary Provisional Government, suggesting that

> they belonged for the most part to the *lumpenproletariat*, which, in all the big towns, form a mass strictly differentiated from the industrial proletariat, a recruiting grounds for thieves and criminals of all kinds, living on the crumbs of society, people without a definite trade, vagabonds, *gens sans feu and sans aveu*, with differences according to the degree of civilization of the nation to which they belong, but never renouncing their *lazzaroni* [hoboes] character.[6]

This litany of not easily "classed" elements does not quite directly evoke African social conditions, though it points at a somewhat similar urban social milieu. To begin with, a much more gender sensitive and diverse listing of urban dwellers would now be required; women, for example, are quite crucial players in Africa both amongst the semi-proletarianized and within the cadre of urban socio-political actors than Marx and Engels' itemization would help us to infer. But note, more generally, the fact that the term lumpenproletariat itself cannot – and certainly should not – be so dismissively employed (not least with reference to the South African case). Not that the more settled and more organized working class need ever be displaced as a particularly central vector of possible progressive promise, of course. Marx himself was the key thinker in emphasizing – and for good reason – the extent to which the concentration and centralization of this "working class" were crucial determinations of its potential socialist aspirations and endeavours – and, indeed, in Africa and elsewhere the consciousness and organizational presence of the working-class has

---

5   Karl Marx, *The 18th Brumaire of Louis Bonaparte* (New York: International Publishers, 1963), p. 75.

6   Karl Marx, *Class Struggles in France* (New York: International Publishers, 1964), p. 50; as he continues, "at the youthful age at which the Provisional Government recruited them [they were] thoroughly malleable, capable of the most heroic deeds and the most exalted sacrifices, as of the basest banditry and the dirtiest corruption."

often been central both to anti-colonial struggles and to resistances to contemporary recolonization. Yet, as we shall see, the number of persons, in their diversity, that the congested urban settings Africa have increasingly to offer can also produce vital expressions of political energy in their own right – these pressing beyond the conceptual boundaries of working class action more conventionally defined and finding voice in particularly dramatic ways (as we have seen most recently in Cairo and in Tunis, for example). To this reality we will have to return.

It is also true that there is stratification *within* this vast mass[7] – shades of difference, difference that can nonetheless have pertinent socio-political effects amongst those "below" the elite and affluent. Such divisions within this lower tier of society itself can be quite diverse in provenance, and can have, for both good and ill, a wide range of expressions: contestations between criminal and victim for example, or between those differentially defined in terms of gender, or diverse ethnic, national (think of the recent xenophobic excesses that have scarred South Africa, for example), and religious affiliation. Nonetheless, where full-time employment is a (relative) "luxury" and the availability of working-class organizations of self-defense a rarity, divisions within the urban mass along socio-economic lines can also be important: not least between the fully employed who are generally more effectively organized at the work-site than are those who are more marginalized, "precarious" and often less well-organized for worker and popular self-defense. Many decades ago Giovanni Arrighi and I actually employed, albeit somewhat controversially, the term "labour aristocracy" (for want of a better phrase) precisely to distinguish these "upper echelons" of the poor (those relatively stabilized in employment) from

---

7   Self-evidently, this reference to the stratification within the proletariat/precariat mass does not refer to the more obvious kind of class differentiation in African settings, that between the upper and most favoured echelons of Africa's hierarchy (the most affluent of owners, politicians and state functionaries, and enterprise managers and their attendant retinues) and those below them on the social ladder; such class differentiations are generally clear enough.

those much more marginalized from capital's activities than themselves.[8] So controversial was this application of the term that I soon after (1975) felt myself forced to clarify and to qualify our use of the term – though I first reestablish our earlier point:

> The "more privileged" and better organized workers have been encouraged to iden-
> tify upward – to become partners (albeit the most junior of partners) in the jos-
> tling for surpluses among the internationally and domestically powerful (includ-
> ing more prominently in the latter category the elites and sub-elites themselves)
> – rather than to identify downward with the even more "wretched of the earth": the
> urban marginals and the average inhabitant of the…rural areas.[9]

But, I quickly added, in a capitalism in crisis the "classic strengths of the urban working class" could become "more evident," with "the up-per stratum of the workers [then] most likely to identify downward [to become] a leading force within a revolutionary alliance of exploited ele-ments in the society." And I also conceded that, in any case, the concept "labour aristocracy" – whether its usage had once been "sanctioned" (in his *Imperialism: The Highest Stage of Capitalism*) by Lenin or not – seemed a harsh one to apply to workers in Africa who remain, to this day, exploited and even more "relatively" disempowered and impoverished vis-à-vis the dominant circles of their societies than they are "relatively" empowered and privileged vis-à-vis their fellow denizens of society's lower orders. In-deed, as one of my current South African correspondents, Eddie Webster,[10] notes (as quoted in the immediately preceding chapter) there may be "more evidence for the concept's appropriateness now;" at the same time he also speaks strongly to this same point, thinking, to repeat, that its use

---

8   In Arrighi and Saul (*op. cit.*).

9   See my "The 'Labour Aristocracy' Thesis Reconsidered" in Richard Sandbrook and
     Robin Cohen (eds.) *The Development of an African Working Class* (Toronto and
     London: University, 1975) and, with the same title but in a somewhat modified
     version, as chapter 12 in *The State and Revolution in Eastern Africa* (London and
     New York: Heinemann and Monthly Review Press, 1975).

10   Eddie Webster, personal communication. I have also cited this suggestive commu-
     nication in my concluding chapter in Saul and Bond, (*op. cit.*).

is "misleading because neoliberal globalization is eroding the core of the labour market, making this 'elite' itself very precarious." Moreover and "secondly, even these core jobs are often below R2000 per month; and, thirdly, almost all workers share their income with a household with an average of five members." And yet, as we also know, such differences as do distinguish these "lower orders" (as Webster adds: "to have job at all in these times may be seen as a privilege rather than a curse"!) can also make for some real differences in terms of divergent "class practices."

As a result, if we carefully frame any such "divergences" of interests and actions with reference to their social basis and to such matters as differential remuneration and job security and differing degrees of effective self-organization, they can be understood to likely have tangible political weight in their implications. And this is true not merely within the working class, between the "settled" proletariat and the more precariously employed. But it is even more true as between those of both these categories of proletariat and those of the urban "precariat" even more broadly defined – as further examination of the South African case will amply confirm. For the politics of the urban dwellers *per se* as distinct from those of the urban proletariat (there is some obvious overlap between categories of course, nor should their likely preoccupations be seen as being necessarily contradictory) can have a quite distinctive dynamic and thrust of its own. For the realm of the precariat is that of "street level politics" – as focussed upon so effectively by Jonathan Barker, among others. A sharp debate has arisen, it might be noted, as to what is the precise import of such "street-level politics"[11] – not so much, be it noted, "workers take to the streets" as "street-dwellers take to the streets." But what we can say is that in such social circumstances is to be found a "people" available for socio-political upsurge (in both township and rural settings). True their actions will perhaps be directed most forcefully at the state and the polity, their programmes and their minions, rather than, directly, at employers.

---

11   See Jonathan Barker, *Street-Level Politics* (Toronto: Between the Lines, 1999).

Perhaps, too, this latter kind of action is not quite as likely to readily expand into socialist challenge as is the workplace-centred confrontations of more formally "proletarian" provenance. And yet even translating workplace confrontation into socialist-style skepticism about, and hostility towards, capitalism *per se* takes creative political and ideological work to help it to happen. How much more of such work is necessary to blend the two worlds of working-class/workplace protest and of urban-rooted protest into resistance at the highest level of clarity and consciousness – even if the varied resistances do implicity set themselves against the same broader reality of capitalist control over, and definition of, the logic of the particular social milieu that provides the context of struggle. If we were to expand our definition of potentially revolutionary resistance to include both working-class and "township" fronts of struggle, is something in danger of being lost – namely, the kind of systemic, more formally "proletarian," struggle, most often brought into confrontational focus at the workplace level. But were Marx and Engels actually correct in seeing "precarious politics" as being primarily "dangerous,"[12] rather than as often being proto-revolutionary. Or is it not, in fact, entirely possible to see these two worlds of resistance and protest as having the potential to relate to and to reinforce each other? If so, and to become entirely concrete, we might then ask of contemporary South Africa how we might hope to see the mix of proletarian and precarian resistances that are so clearly visible being

---

12 Dangerous? As I complete this piece I learn, via the internet, of a new book by Guy Standing set to appear, one entitled *The Precariat: The New Dangerous Class* – thus underscoring in one title both concepts I deploy here: "the precariat" and "the dangerous class." Clearly Standing and I are working along some similar lines since, beyond the title itself, the flyer I have received announcing the book's launch summarizes its content as follows: "The Precariat is a new class, comprising the growing number of people facing lives of insecurity, doing work without a past or future. Their lack of belonging and identity means inadequate access to social and economic rights. Why is this new class growing, what political dangers does it represent and how might these be addressed?" I have yet to read this still forthcoming publication of course, but, while intrigued, I am rather surprised to hear only "dangers" being mentioned in its announcement (above). The reality on the ground is much more complicated (and more promising) in South Africa.

blended into a coherent and cumulatively counter-hegemonic project of genuinely socialist and democratic provenance.

My own conclusion (but see also chapter 6 below): this circle can and must be squared. For there are certainly proletarians and even semi-proletarians in the Global South generally (and in South Africa more specifically) who can come to develop a working-class consciousness that permits them to understand that their grievances as regards their specific employers should, even more fundamentally, be directed against the capitalist system itself. And there is also "a people" – poor people, marginalized in both urban and rural settings – who are as capable of socio-political upsurge as those engaged in socio-economic confrontation at the workplace; these latter can perhaps be called an "under-class"/pre-cariat (or even, in a far more metaphorical and much less scientific way, seen as members of "the working-class"). In short, a politics that seeks to engage in a broad-based mobilization of both proletariat and precariat could indeed, if mounted deftly, have cumulative, very real and entirely positive revolutionary potential.

II. Lagos and Beyond:
The Politics of "Precarious" Settings

What, in such terms, of Africa? The continent presents an increasingly urban setting certainly, cities growing exponentially throughout the continent – with the population of places like Lagos or Cairo already reaching quite staggering proportions. Of course, this is a global phenomenon, as George Packer writes in an article on Lagos entitled "The Megacity", of the Global South more generally:

> Around a billion people – almost half of the developing world's urban population – live in slums. The United Nations Human Settlements Program, in a 2003 report titled "The Challenge of the Slums," declared, "The urban poor are trapped in an informal and 'illegal' world – in slums that are not reflected on maps, where waste is not collected, where taxes are not paid, and where public services are not provided. Officially, they do not exist." According to the report, "Over the course of the next

two decades, the global urban population will double, from 2.5 to 5 billion. Almost all of this increase will be in developing countries."[13]

But Packer's main focus is Africa and, particularly, what is, for him, a megacity par excellence: Lagos in Nigeria. In that city, as he reminds us, "in 1950, fewer than three hundred thousand people lived [there]." [However, he continues,] "in the second half of the twentieth century, the city grew at a rate of more than six percent annually. It is currently the sixth-largest city in the world, and it is growing faster than any of the world's other megacities (the term used by the United Nations Center for Human Settlements for 'urban agglomerations' with more than ten million people). By 2015, it is projected, Lagos will rank third, behind Tokyo and Bombay, with twenty-three million inhabitants." And it is in such cities that "urban dwellers" can become socio-economic actors in ways that may far transcend the proletarian and semi-proletarian descriptors that in past reality applied to at least some of them – and this can sometimes have quite radical implications.

Working-class? Yes and no. Thus, as Freund once wrote of Africa:

> While it might seem at first sight that urbanization and direct subjection to market production would have brought about a class of workers that could be relatively easily understood and subsumed under the categories of capitalist industrial society familiar to Westerners there are problems…in comprehending labour…in the African city…Only a small section of African workers actually are wage workers operating in the sphere of mass commodity production. Nor is this section growing very significantly.[14]

Indeed, says Freund, "a conservative…estimate of the working population of the Nigerian metropolis of Lagos in the 1970s suggested that only a minority is to be found registered as wage workers." True, Freund's argument here antedates emergence of the more recent and truly mammoth Lagos evoked in a preceding paragraph. But the same point

---

13   George Packer, "The Megacity," *The New Yorker*, (Nov. 13, 2006).

14   Bill Freund, *The African Worker* (Cambridge and New York: Cambridge University Press, 1988).

doubtless still holds. What is one to make of this "mass," sometimes epitomized as the "informal sector"? As Freund continues,

> The state in colonial times and often thereafter has taken an ambiguous stance at best towards the "informal" sector of the economy and those who work within it. Classic development theories focussed on industrialization and its consequences in an urban context or the development of a prosperous peasantry in a rural one. The world of shanty towns, of corner stalls and makeshift sweatshops, of women selling little packets of flavouring for stew, individual cigarettes and bars of soap do not belong to the structures that it proposed and planned. It is supposed to be a mark of backwardness and a temporary phenomenon only. In reality, though, it is precisely the 'informal sector' that has flourished most in post-colonial Africa and any serious assessment of the African workers has to give it a serious share of attention.[15]

In fact, Peter Gutkind had anticipated this point in an earlier analysis. Under colonialism, he stated, urbanization could only "produce a 'marginal' urban population who live in precarious conditions, exploited in one form or another by the dominant colonial group and relegated ecologically to the peripheries of towns and economically to the peripheries of a producing and consuming society." Indeed, he continued, the African city is best seen as being "made up of three basic population groups, a plebian urban mob, workers and artisans."[16] True, Gutkind saw fit to characterize this heterogeneous urban population as having a kind of broad-gauged proletarian consciousness. Again, "yes and no" must be the most accurate response, proletarian consciousness becoming, in such a formulation and as noted earlier, as much a metaphor as a precise scientific description. For what, we must ask, does such "proletarian consciousness" actually amount to, especially since post-colonial urban Africa has not been so fundamentally altered structurally from its earlier colonial profile. No wonder that many have felt forced to understand in fresh ways the complexities of an unfinished transition to a cleanly and clearly defined (and polarized)

15   Freund, *ibid.*

16   Peter Gutkind, *The poor in urban Africa: a prologue to modernization, conflict and the unfinished revolution* (Montreal: McGill University Centre for Developing Areas Studies, 1968).

capitalist-based society that might otherwise be thought to merely stymie revolutionary aspiration in present-day Africa? Thus observers like Post and Wright have persisted in taking a high road in their understanding of those social elements set adrift by a failed capitalist "transformation." They take a first step in allowing our sense of class contradictions – and of class belonging – to be markedly expanded, especially with respect to Africa and the rest of the Global South. For there, in societies profoundly altered but not transformed by the impact of capitalism, the roster of those exploited (and potentially available for apparently class-based action) is far wider than narrow "classist" categories can hope to elucidate – and this is not just to speak of all those peasants out there! Hence their key formulation:

> The working out of capitalism in parts of the periphery prepares not only the mi-
> nority working class but peasants and other working people, women, youth and
> minorities for a socialist solution, even though the political manifestation of this
> may not initially take the form of a socialist movement. In the case of those who are
> *not* wage labourers (the classical class associated with that new order) capitalism
> has still so permeated the social relations which determine their existences, even
> though it may not have followed the western European pattern of "freeing" their
> labour power, that to be liberated from it is their only salvation. The objective need
> for socialism of these elements can be no less than that of the worker imprisoned in
> the factory and disciplined by the whip of unemployment. The price [of capitalism]
> is paid in even the most "successful" of the underdeveloped countries, and oth-
> ers additionally experience mass destitution. Finding another path has...become
> a desperate necessity if the alternative of continuing, if not increasing, barbarism
> is to be escaped.[17]

Yet even this may not quite go far enough. Such forces do indeed struggle for equality, but, be it noted, not necessarily and in the first instance for socialism. This is the maelstrom of struggles that we have seen Jonathan Barker epitomize in his writing[18] as constituting a world of protest and resistance that stretches beyond the workplace and often

---

17   Ken Post and Phil Wright, *Socialism and Underdevelopment* (London and New
      York: Routledge, 1989), pp. 151–152.

18   Jonathan Barker, *op. cit.*, p. 13.

elaborates its politics in terms that are not quite so easily recognized as "progressive" in the most conventional of Marxist terms. Yet should we not look for our systemic contradictions where we find them. Barker, for example, sees the phenomenon he refers to as a "social response to the expansion of market logic into social relationships that have more than economic meaning to people." And elsewhere he speaks of the existence, in Africa and beyond, of "thousands of activist groups addressing the issues of housing, functioning of local markets, availability of local social services, provision and standard of education and abusive and damaging working conditions."[19] As suggested above, this does not mean that it will be easy to get the poor, both urban and rural, to see their negative situations in effectively proletarian and anti-capitalist terms. After all, the vector of oppression these poor often feel most tangibly is that of the state, the state that has been designated to police a semi-transformed society, and often, as well, to refuse, on behalf of capital and the locally powerful, legitimate popular claims for social services and social redress. Hence the tendency for the poor and the "untransformed" to give at least as much importance to "street-level politics" as to workplace contestation in defining the overall texture of their political aspirations and actions.

Indeed, I would argue, it is precisely under such conditions that the left must feel compelled, much more imaginatively than ever before (in terms of clear principle and by means of compromise and assiduous political work), to seek to draw the best of various claims and assertions (both street-corner and work-site) as arise from diverse but closely related contradictions into effectively counter-hegemonic projects.[20] These

19   Jonathan Barker, "Debating Globalization: Critique of Colin Leys," *Southern Africa Report (SAR)*, 12, 4 [September, 1997]).

20   Note that Barker himself is skeptical about the priority (or even wisdom) of seeking to discover some counter-hegemony to encompass and generalize the diversity of such important and legitimate claims. On this aspect of the question he is effectively answered, in my opinion, in *Southern Africa Report*, by Colin Leys, "Colin Leys Replies," *SAR*, 12, 4 (September, 1997) and Veronica Schild, "Their Hegemony or Ours," *SAR*, 3, 4 (August, 1998).

must become, in short, claims and assertions that represent the "highest common factor" of their protagonists' various social locations. Of course, these will certainly include workers' specific shop-floor demands but the poor more generally can be mobilized across quite a broad front and behind a kind of revolutionary and eminently progressive populism that brings them to defy not only oppression *per se* but also, tendentially, the rule of capital itself. For we quite simply cannot stop at a more expansive class definition of agency. Instead, we must also make a positive force in our struggle for liberation of other tensions in society that can be wed to claims and assertions advanced in the name of class-defined redress if we are imaginative enough to do so.

Indeed, as my former teacher and old friend Ralph Miliband has noted, capitalism's grossly uneven development around the world has produced "extremely fertile terrain" for the kind of "pathological deformations" – predatory authoritarianisms and those "demagogues and charlatans peddling their poisonous wares...of ethnic and religious exclusion and hatred"[21] – that now scar the global landscape. As I would add: losing confidence in socialist and other humanely modern, humanely cooperative, projects, people turn for social meaning to more ready-to-hand identities, often with fundamentalist fervour. And yet, despite this, progressives committed to class struggle can and should continue to view such identities as contingent in their socio-political implications and as not being, in most cases, in contradiction with socialist purposes. And we should, when possible, invite the bearers of such identities – alongside feminists, environmentalists, anti-racists, activists around issues of sexual orientation and the like – to join us within a broader community-in-the-making and within a universalizing democratic project of global, anti-capitalist transformation. In fact, as Miliband continues,

> ...everywhere there are common goals and aspirations – for democratic forms where they are denied and for more democratic forms where these are no more

---

21   Ralph Miliband, *Socialism in a Sceptical Age* (London: Verso, 1995), p. 192.

than a screen for oligarchic rule; for the achievement of a social order in which improvements in the condition of the most deprived – often a majority of the population – is the prime concern of governments; for the subordination of the economy to meeting social needs. In all countries, there are people, in numbers large and small, who are moved by the vision of a new social order in which democracy, egalitarianism and cooperation – the essential values of socialism – would be prevailing principles of social organization. It is in the growth of their numbers and in the success of their struggles that lies the best hope for humankind.[22]

And a corollary of this position is equally compelling: we on the left had better learn to operate in our complex world of diverse faiths, races and ethnic belongings, to unite such "belongings" to our cause of class liberation, or they will continue to return to haunt us – as "merely" divisive "identifiers" and claims that can, at their worst, turn rancid and dangerous to humane purpose. So, too, must gender-defined and environmentally-concerned projects be ever more assertively articulated as being, not reducible to, but coequal with and enlarged by an assertion of class considerations.[23] In short, one of our key goals must be to define "agency" not merely in terms of some rather abstractly defined "working class interest." For that apparently simple slogan – correct but excessively schematic – has presented far too open an invitation to arrogance and high-handedness (in the interest of the "working class," don't you know) to essentialist vanguards of all kinds, ever quick to assert arrogantly just what "the class" must and should do. Instead we need to reach towards the range of shades of identity within and beyond strict class boundaries that can be won to revolutionary praxis. Not that tensions between diverse goals and purposes will then simply disappear, of course. Yet seeking to realize such an enlarged project of "class struggle" also underlines the requirement of much more democratic methods of negotiation of both the means and the ends of revolutionary work than has characterized

---

22   *Ibid.*, pp. 194–195.

23   Material in this paragraph is drawn from my book *Development after Globalization* (*op. cit.*), especially ch. 3, "Identifying Class, Classifying Difference," where this overall argument is spelled out at much greater length.

most past socialist undertakings – in mobilizing the forces both to launch revolutionary change and to sustain the process of socialist construction in the long run.

III. South Africa:
Proletariat and Precariat

Here South Africa is a key case, one that I examine at greater length in chapters 4 and 6. Therefore, to complete the present chapter I will merely sketch something of that analysis in order further to clarify the more general argument being made here while also referring the reader forward to chapter 6. For the fact is that South Africa is the country in Africa that has experienced a more "modern" and conventionally capitalist transformation than the rest of the continent – and it has had a greater degree of a recognizable "proletarianization," due, in particular, to its dramatic (and on-going) "mineral revolution" of the past 150 years. But it is also a society marked by the perpetuation and further growth of that "dangerous class" of which we have spoken (those mired, especially in the vast urban townships, in the swamp of "precarious work"...and less). It is certainly true, for example, that the organized working class has been a key player in the country's politics – a major player, for example, at the intersection of class struggle and anti-apartheid assertion.[24] It was, in fact, the crucial

---

24   The documentation on this subject is substantial but for a useful overview of CO-
      SATU and the organized working-class as it emerged into the post-apartheid mi-
      lieu and a "neo-liberalizing world" see Eddie Webster and Glenn Adler, "Exodus
      Without a Map: The Labour Movement in a Liberalizing South Africa" in Bjorn
      Beckman and Lloyd Sachikonye (eds.) *Labour Regimes and Liberalization: The
      Restructuring of State-Society Relations in Africa* (Harare: University of Zimba-
      bwe Press, 2001). See also, for an analysis of more recent developments, Roger
      Southall and Eddie Webster, "Unions and parties in South Africa: COSATU and
      the ANC in the wake of Polokwane" in Bjorn Beckman, Sakhela Buhlungu and
      Lloyd Sachikonye (eds.), *Trade Unions and Party Politics: Labour Movements in
      Africa* (Cape Town: HSRC Press, 2010) and, inter alia, Carolyn Bassett and Marlea
      Clarke, "South African trade unions and globalization: going for the 'high-road,'
      getting stuck on the 'low-road,'" *World Organization, Labour and Globalization*, v.
      2, # 1(Spring, 2008) and Sakhela Buhlungu, *A Paradox of Victory: COSATU and the*

role played by COSATU as it emerged as the key centre of organized black labour in the 1980s that gave observers, who were skeptical from quite early on as to the revolutionary credentials of the ANC/SACP the sense that something more radical was afoot in South Africa. But of course the promise was even wider than that epitomized by COSATU, for it also lay in the broader movement of township-based self-assertion on the part of many Africans of different genders and diverse social locations. Though this kind of popular assertion was not facilitated by the ANC's reassertion of its vanguardist mind-set during its ascension to power,[25] it was to revive in opposition to the policies of state and ruling party in the 1990s and, especially, in the first decade of the new century.

Now, in fact, some have begun to see the possibility of the dawning of a new kind of self-conscious joining of workplace and street-level assertions of the kind that had – thanks to the saliency and universality of apartheid as shared enemy – underpinned broad-based struggles in the 1980s. True, the best organized workers did often seem remarkably deaf to the promise of counter-hegemonic struggle, having apparently pledged themselves, from quite early on, to the role of junior partner (as "quasi-labour aristocrats"?) to the ANC/SACP as part of the Tripartite Alliance in objective support of a neo-liberal overall trajectory for the economy.[26] And the manifestations of township struggle, despite the wide-spread nature of their expression, remain paradoxical as well. For as regards the broad mass of the impoverished we find a population locked, on the one hand, in almost slavish electoral thrall to the ANC and its lliberation-struggle

---

Democratic Transformation in South Africa (Scottsville, S.A: University of KwaZulu-Natal Press, 2010).

25   See Rusty Bernstein's revealing 2002 letter to the author, later published as "The turning point... Letter from Rusty Bernstein to John S. Saul" in *Transformation*, #64 (2007).

26   On the virtues of a new "small-a" alliance between organized labour and civil society, one that could deplace the presently existing "large-A" Alliance from political centrality in South Africa, see John S. Saul, *Revolutionary Traveller* (*op. cit.*), pp. 292–296 and Patrick Bond, "South African splinters" (*op. cit.*).

credentials – while, on the other hand, it is also a population ready to act out, at "street-level" as it were and in highly dramatic fashion, its resistance to a broad range of governmental policies and activities. Thus, in his recent important article on what he terms to be the "Rebellion of the Poor", Peter Alexander has argued that:

> Since 2004 South Africa has experienced a movement of local protests amounting to a rebellion of the poor. This has been widespread and intense, reaching insurrectionary proportions in some cases. On the surface, the protests have been about service delivery and against uncaring, self-serving corrupt leaders of the municipalities. A key feature has been mass participation by a new generation of fighters, especially unemployed youth but also school students. Many issues that underpinned the [initial] ascendency of Jacob Zuma also fuel the present action, including a sense of injustice arising from the realities of persistent inequality.[27]

As he futher notes, "While the inter-connections between the local protest, and between the local protests and militant action involving other elements of civil society, are limited, it is suggested that this is likely to change"! Note, finally, that there are two main schools of thought as to how to conceive the "class belonging" of such an array of protest in contemporary South Africa. One, clearly exemplified by David Harvey and Patrick Bond in their writings, sees in the energies evidenced by these and other assertions of "civil society" the manifestation of a genuinely proletarian reality of struggle – struggle directly linked to other tangibly workplace-centered actions by those of more familiar working-class belonging. For such writers of the left, Gillian Hart suggests, "the central task is to rip away the mask that obfuscates neoliberal class power [confident that] such an exposé will help pave the way for a coherent resurgence of mass movements...[moving] beyond race, ethnicity, gender, and other dimensions of difference in order to achieve class-based solidarity in an increasingly dangerous world."[28] But this is not quite good enough, Hart asserts.

---

27   Peter Alexander, "Rebellion of the poor: South Africa's service delivery protests – a preliminary analysis," *Review of African Political Economy*, v. 37, #123 (March, 2010).

28   Gillian Hart, "Provocations of neoliberalism: Contesting the nation and liberation

As for Hart's own position, she then writes:

> *Pace* David Harvey, the task confronting the left in South Africa and elsewhere is considerably more complex than that of exposing neoliberal class power. Nor is it adequate to posit a shift from race to class apartheid. Most immediately, the ANC government's embrace of GEAR constitutes a re-articulation of race and class that is also part of an activist project of rule.[29]

Note this last sentence: "class," "race," "rule" (and, in another context, she would no doubt add "gender"); small wonder that, for her, "the challenges facing the left are far more complex" than, in her view, Harvey cares to countenance.

> The drama that exploded at Polokwane [site of Zuma's challenging of Mbeki] was as much about contesting the meaning of nation and liberation as it was about the fallout from a neoliberal class project and socio-economic structure and we ignore these sentiments and struggles at our peril.[30]

In sum, she is saying, the claims of a left-populism[31] that self-consciously takes the liberatory claims centered on considerations of gender, race and the exercise of democratic voice with great seriousness, must not be obscured by any too exclusive a preoccupation with the simultaneous reality of class determination.

How best, to repeat, to square this particular circle: "class politics" vs. "a more broadly liberatory politics?" The short answer: both of the above. For the Bonds and the Harts are equally correct, as far as they go. However, it is in making the two pieces of the puzzle – the puzzle as to what can and will drive the "lower orders" in their pursuit of equity – fit together for revolutionary purposes that the real challenge lies. It is easy

---

after apartheid" in Brij Maharaj, Ashwin Desai and Patrick Bond (eds.), *Zuma's Own Goal: Losing South Africa's 'War on Poverty'* (Trenton, N.J.: African World Press, 2011), p. 82.

29   Hart, *ibid.*, p. 83. Bond's own characteristic mode of argument is epitomized by Hart, *ibid.*, p. 96.

30   Hart, *ibid.*, p. 96.

31   This is not a phrase that Hart herself uses, it should be noted.

to see how they might not fit: the most organized of workers going deeper and deeper into the (minimally) gilded ghetto of "privilege;" township dwellers more and more seduced down the blind-alleys of the most "dangerous" of consciousnesses: criminality, xenophobia, ethnic rivalry and the like.[32] But, on both sides of the equation, such postures remain so far from being the whole story of workplace and township life that many South African activists reach for a different narrative, a different possibility. Add to this the fact that, on both sides of the equation claims are, at their best, driven by a demand for equity and fairness, disturbingly liberal-sounding substantives in their vague and potentially windy abstraction, but words with meaning nonetheless. And one thing more: the varied terrains of struggle need each other. For "class" preoccupations pursued without full attention to the terrains of struggle for gender and racial equality and for a guarantee of access to the expression of real democratic voice are as unlikely to make a meaningful revolution as are movements based on gender, race and voice that don't take demands based on class considerations sufficiently seriously.[33] Genuine liberation, genuine socialism, genuine liberatory socialism demand all four components of these multiple components – and others besides, notably environmental concerns for example.

---

32   See John S. Saul, "Race, Class, Gender and Voice" (*op. cit.*).

33   The complexities of township life, the realities of a real struggle for equity there, and the simultaneous danger of slippage to less than savoury outcomes have been well documented in recent literature. But see, in addition to Peter Alexander (as cited in footnote 26), the running compilations of township unrest being assembled by John Devenish at the University of KwaZulu/Natal. See too such fine "township insider" accounts as that by Jacob Dlamini and entitled *Native Nostalgia* (Aukland Park, S.A.: Jacana, 2009), a book at once sociological and autobiographical.

CHAPTER 6

CONCLUSIONS

The Struggle Really Does Continue in Southern Africa

It is important to look at the regional struggle for the freedom of southern Africa in a global context for such a perspective helps to underscore the unique importance of the set of events that transpired there. Put simply, this regional struggle (involving, from 1960 to 1994, the contested territories of Angola, Mozambique, South-West Africa/Namibia, Rhodesia/Zimbabwe and South Africa) marked the last major battle-ground of a much broader struggle waged across the globe for the overthrow of western colonialism and white racist hegemony, a struggle that spanned the twentieth century and that was perhaps the most significant event of that century.

Section A of this final chapter will, in its first sub-section, set out both the global and continental terms of this latter assertion (and its relevant qualifications) historically and analytically – while also reprising the concepts of an "Empire of Capital" and "recolonization" that I have found, both in this book and in other of my recent writings, usefully to frame a specification of present-day realities in the Global South. A further sub-section will again – though at greater length than in earlier chapters – evoke the work of Frantz Fanon (but also that of Amilcar Cabral) to help refine the focus of my general approach to Africa itself. I will then proceed in subsequent subsections to synthesize what has been written in this book regarding the southern region of Africa itself, viewing this region as having been both the final redoubt of an overt colonial (and white rule) presence on the continent and also the final site of the broader world-wide anti-colonial struggle that we are, in the first instance, evoking here.

As we will have to remind ourselves in a concluding section (C) the hopes for a resurgent struggle to more meaningfully "liberate" each of the ostensibly-liberated countries of southern Africa are far from buoyant ones – though this is perhaps least true in South Africa itself (which is also the home of the region's most developed economy). Before proceeding to this final brief reflection on region-wide considerations, a second section (B) will seek to examine some recent South African responses to the grim realities in that country in its "post-apartheid" period. Here I will quote at some length from several active South African players (from vocal entrepreneur Moeletsi Mbeki, from trade-union leader Zwelinzima Vavi, and from activists of one emergent counter-hegemonic alternative to the ANC, the Democratic Left Front/DLF, for example), to give some flavour of the discussions of the moment there.

And I will conclude this second section with some mention of the Marikana Massacre of August 16, 2012 when some 36 miners engaged in peaceful industrial action were gunned down by the state's police. This incident has been described in mainstream accounts as "the single most lethal use of force by South African security forces against civilians since 1990 and the end of the apartheid era" (an account that goes on, it is worth underscoring, to observe that "the shootings have been described as a massacre in the South African media and have been compared to Sharpeville massacre in 1960").[1] Mention of the Marikana outrage here

---

1　Wikipedia, "The Marikana miners' strike" (accessed online, February, 2013). As this account continues, "Controversy emerged after it was discovered that most of the victims were shot in the back and many victims were shot far from police lines," and it concludes that "the Strike is considered a seminal event in modern South African history, and was followed by similar strikes at other mines across South Africa, events which have collectively made 2012 the most protest filled year in the country since the end of apartheid."

will be necessarily brief however, since Marikana is covered in much more detail in another recent book that I have co-authored with Patrick Bond and entitled *South Africa – The Present as History: From Mrs Ples to Marikana*. There, as noted in my introduction to the present volume, two detailed conclusions focus primarily on the events at Marikana, seen in both historical and contemporary perspective and to which the reader of the present volume may be referred.[2] Here we will conclude, as promised, with a briefly stated characterization of the Southern African region's recent history, of its present moment and its possible future anticipated above.

A. The Southern African Victory: Liberation Realized or Prelude to Recolonization?[3]

1. A Global Contestation

But recall here the formulation in our opening paragraph: anti-colonialism and world-wide decolonization as the "most significant event of the entire century"? It is true that the 20th century had seen, among other things, the confirmation of the ascendancy of the economic might and seemingly boundless power of the United States; the Russian Revolution and the rise and fall of the Soviet Union; the reawakening under Communist rule of China and that country's march back to global prominence; the horrors of Hitler and his Holocaust; and two "World Wars" of stunning inhumanity waged at frightful cost. And yet Southern Africa was the culmination of something at least as noteworthy – and yet all too easy, it would seem, for orthodox historians to overlook or to underestimate.[4] After all, in the

---

2   Saul and Bond, *op. cit.*

3   The section (A) of the chapter appears, in much the same form, and with the same title as the present section bears, as "The Southern African Victory: Liberation Realized or a Prelude to Recolonization?" in *Radical History Review*, Vol. 14, #119 (Spring, 2014).

4   But see, *inter alia*, Mark Crocker, *Rivers of Blood, Rivers of Gold: Europe's Conquest of Indigenous Peoples* (New York: Grove Press, 1997); Sophie Bessis, *Western Supremacy: The Triumph of an Idea* (London: Zed Books, 2003); Vijay Prashad, *The Darker Nations: A People's History of the Third World* (New York: The New Press,

year 1939, 13 million square miles and almost 500 million members of the globe's population lay under the domination of the West's economic and political power – thanks to the centuries-old frenzy for conquest and enforced colonization indulged in by Western Europe.[5] Moreover, the overweening racism and cultural hubris of the white inhabitants of that same "West" were both entangled with and further amplified by such a process of global conquest.

And yet by the end of the century the authoritarian structures of the once overpowering colonial overlordship spawned by "the Great White West" – structures that served almost exclusively to further the latter's own interests – had, quite simply, been effaced. Indeed, one is forced to recall W. E. B. DuBois' ringing 1903 prophecy: "The problem of the twentieth century is the problem of the color-line – the relation of the darker to the lighter races of men in Asia and Africa, in America and the islands of the sea."[6] And the upshot of that "problem"? DuBois' "darker races" – "the darker nations" as Vijay Prashad has more recently also termed them[7] – had fought back against their oppressors in the latter half of the twentieth century and, no longer as part of the problem but as part of the solution, had won.

And won? Well, not quite. For there was rather more to western global power than racism, however important that dimension was in its own right. There was also the aforementioned fact that western imperialism was motivated in its rise to global prominence not only by white arro-

---

2007) and Sven Lindqvist, *"Exterminate All the Brutes": One Man's Odyssey into the Heart of Darkness and the Origins of European Genocide* (New York: The New Press, 1996); for a pertinent regional study see Walter Rodney, *How Europe Underdeveloped Africa* (London and Dar es Salaam: Bogle l'Overture Publications and Tanzania Publishing House, 1972).

5   Thomas Benjamin (ed.), "Preface" to *The Encyclopedia of Western Colonialism Since 1450* (New York: Macmillan Reference USA, 2005).

6   In W. E. B. Du Bois' introduction (entitled "The Forethought") to his *The Souls of Black Folk* (New York: New American Library, 1903), p. 19.

7   Prashad, *op. cit.*; his phrase "the darker nations" characterizes a "non-white world" in a much more positive, pro-active phrase than "non-white," referring to people who are, more positively (and proudly), "brown," "yellow," "black" and other tones.

gance, Christian hubris and profound cultural insensitivity. No, it also had at core firm economic motives spawned by a capitalist socio-economic system that first found its feet in Western Europe and then, slowly but surely, reached out its multiple tentacles to embrace the world. It was on this stage, of course, that the epic drama of successful anti-colonialism was also to play itself out. Yet it is the case that, even as the firmly racist structures (exemplified by direct colonial domination) were peeled back, much of the economic basis of the West's predominance was still in place at the end of the decolonization process – framing a system that many were soon to term "neo-colonialism."

In this format of domination the United States – itself the artifact of remorseless capitalist territorial expansion at an earlier stage of its own history[8] – increasingly stood at the centre of the global system of continued capitalist domination and expansion. But the US had much less interest in territorial conquest than it had in economic control of the now ostensibly autonomous countries beyond the North Atlantic core. Realizing its global reach through its powerful corporations and financial organizations – and it willingness to employ, when "necessary," the brute power of its fearsome military machine – it was the US and not the former European centres of formal colonization that became the hub of the "neo-colonialism" that came to hold the Third World in its grip. Indeed the US proved to be the major beneficiary of the very demise of formal colonialism, a demise that now opened the world's borders even more widely to the unchecked expansion of American capitalism's control.[9]

And yet the process of capitalist evolution and the transformation of the parameters of global domination would not stop there. For the im-

---

8   See Crocker, *op. cit.*, especially Part III, "The Dispossession of the Apache" and Richard Drinnon, *Facing West: The Metaphysics of Indian Hating and Empire-Building* (New York: New American Library, 1980).

9   Leo Panitch and Sam Gindin, *The Making of Global Capitalism: The Political Economy of American Empire* (London: Verso Books, 2012). But note the use of both the terms "global capitalism" and "American empire" in the book's title. This was once perhaps an apparent repetition of terms; increasingly, however, the presumed link between these two phrases seems to be ever more a contradiction in terms.

perialism of neo-colonialism was being slowly but surely dépassé in its turn. Thus, if the key to American imperialism in the early post-colonial era was market power articulated on an ostensibly open economic terrain ("open" primarily, it bears emphasizing, to the ever freer run of capital), the fundamental logic at work has continued to roll out to a next stage. To be sure, the combination of US capital and the US state retains a powerful role within the world of capital and its on-going expansion – not least, as noted, because of the importance of American military weight as the "global cop" of last resort. Moreover, "the American empire," as some see fit to term the global capitalist system even now, is policed economically in considerable part by such international organizations as the International Monetary Fund, the World Bank and the G8/G20 in which the United States itself does continue to have preponderant power.

At the same time, however, new contenders for economic primacy have now emerged – including runaway American corporations for whom the new semi-borderless world was to become a major attraction, promising new markets but also cheaper labour at other sites of production around the world than "at home".[10] Equally importantly, newly aggressive staging grounds for capital beyond the familiar North Atlantic centres also began to emerge, and these too increasingly provided new players for the global capitalist game. Japanese interests had already become just such a global player. And now China also began to step ever more assertively into the world's capitalist arena.[11] And so did the capital of Korean, Indian, Brazilian and other provenances.

Thus a newspaper headline of December 11, 2012, that states baldly: "Asian economies to outstrip Western nations by 2030: 'Spectacular rise' of Asia redoing US power, trends report says." And the "trends report" that it is drawing on? It is, in fact, the "Global Trends 2030" released by the National Intelligence Council and, as the article says, "timed for the

---

10   Nayan Chanda, "US Sours on Globalization: Protests may have abated, but global-ization has fewer supporters in the US as job numbers don't add up," *Businessworld*, 25 May 2011.

11   See Giovanni Arrighi, *Adam Smith in Beijing: Lineages of the 21ˢᵗ Century* (London: Verso Press, 2007).

start of the new presidential administration... aimed at helping U.S. policymakers plan for the future." The report's chief thrust: "The United States could see its standing as a super-power eroded and Asian economies will outstrip those of North America and Europe combined by 2030, according to the best guess of the U.S. intelligence community. 'The spectacular rise of Asian economies is dramatically altering U.S. influence,' said Christopher Newton" (Newton being the chair of the N.I.C.).[12] Indeed, a second journalistic account of this report is headlined: "US Intelligence Analysts: American Power is in Terminal Decline"![13]

In short, it is a whole new world of capital that is a-dawning with, increasingly, the diverse nodes of capital themselves defining collectively the imperial project. Of course, such "nodes of capital" have still been dependent, in many ways, on "their" states to help discover just how to both police the overall system and to keep it running smoothly. But – and this is the crucial point – they have also increasingly found a distinctive global weight and substance in their own right. No longer primarily "American capital," or "Canadian capital," or "Chinese capital," or "German capital," or "Indian capital," but ever more united by common (if also divided) interest as a force – the world's predominant force! – in and of itself. Capital: fractured, competitive, and in unresolved tension with differing state structures ("can't live with them and can't live without them!") but bent, nonetheless, on a joint project of further crafting the world in their own image. As something new: an "Empire of Capital."[14]

One further conceptual foray is perhaps necessary here in order further to clear the ground for concrete analysis. Begin with colonialism and then decolonization. But decolonization into a new world of unadorned western capitalist global supremacy no longer premised virtually

---

12   "Asian economies to outstrip Western nations by 2030," *Toronto Star*, December 11, 2012.

13   Dave Lindorff, "US Intelligence Analysts: American Power is in Terminal Decline," Information Clearing House, December 13, 2012.

14   See Ellen Meiksins Wood, *Empire of Capital* (London: Verso, 2003) and my own *Empire and Decolonization: Contesting the Rhetoric and Reality of Resubordination in Southern Africa and Beyond* (Delhi: Three Essays Collective, 2008).

anywhere on the structures of formal colonialism. For, as we have seen, "independence" for the Global South originally had been sited within a powerful global capitalist economy, one defined, in the first instance, by American market-based hegemony. Thus the stage was set for (to repeat) "neo-colonialism." At the same time, this brave new world of free-market imperialism was, at least in principle, non-nation-based, and this in turn meant that the world was now ever more open, theoretically, to a fresh array of capitalist undertakings. True, in much of the Global South (not least in Africa) the theoretical possibility of finding effective traction for an assertive domestic (and globally expansive) capitalism was not always readily available in practice: global capital from the strongest of economies was certainly omnipresent and ready to cream off attractive natural resources, attractive investment opportunities, and the like from the so-called "Third World." But the world was a more competitive place and also more open to the emergence of fledgling rivals from within a dawning Empire of Capital itself. This fact too must be encompassed in our analysis.

2. Fanon, Cabral and Decolonization

What did this mean for those at the receiving end of empire (of various distinct kinds over the decades) in the Global South. Formal colonialism, as referred to above, was one such phase of imperial control certainly. What then of "decolonization"? This latter process was modified, as we have suggested, by the varying economic strengths and weaknesses of the former colonies themselves and by the relative strength of the continuing economic push of the former colonial metropoles of Europe. But most of all it was modified, as stated, by the assertion, in the years following the Second World War, of an ever growing American economic, political and cultural role as neo-colonial power. And the implications for Africa? Here the most powerful theorists of this phase of "post-colonial" history, especially with respect to Africa, were undoubtedly Frantz Fanon and Amilcar Cabral. Indeed, the writings of Fanon (1925–1961) and Cabral (1924–1973) remain, to this day, far more crucial touchstones for understanding Africa's "successful" anti-imperialist struggles and their aftermath than the work of any more academic analyst, then or since.

Take, first, Fanon. He was much the most eloquent critical analyst of phase two of colonialist outreach: the period of "false decolonization"/"neo-colonialism," underscoring clearly the shifting tactics in Africa of established colonial powers like Britain and France as they adjusted to (and helped shape) the realities of a decolonizing world. Particularly important here was their change in the tactics of continued domination; ultimately, when confronted by a rising tide of resistance to colonialism in Africa that threatened to become particularly militant and even proto-revolutionary, they began, finally (and after their earlier disasters in India, Indo-China and Algeria) to consider the possibility of seeking neo-colonial solutions. As Fanon writes of this moment:

> That is why a veritable panic takes hold of the colonialist governments in turn. Their purpose is to capture the vanguard, to turn the movement of liberation to the right and disarm the people, quick, quick, let's decolonize. Decolonize the Congo before it turns into another Algeria. Vote the constitutional framework for all Africa, create the French Communauté, renovate that same Communauté, but for God's sake let's decolonize quick....And they decolonize at such a rate that they [even] impose independence on Houphouet-Boigny.

And "capture the vanguard" they surely did, both to forward their own longer term imperial designs but also to, in effect, forward (whether intentionally or not) the designs of the broader, increasingly American-dominated, world of global capital.

It is true that Fanon did strongly emphasize the reassertion of economic control over particular colonies likely to be asserted by one resurgent ex-colonial power or another (France or the UK, principally). But, as the previous paragraph hints, he knew that something else was afoot too: the ever greater importance of the overall hegemony of global capitalism and, in particular, the shift in power within that capitalist world and its free market imperialism towards the growing centrality of the United States. As he states, "in this fresh juncture the Americans take their role of patron of international capitalism very seriously" – the US pressing the waning European masters of direct colonialism towards a

faster pace in decolonization than they might have fashioned for themselves. It was this reality that would help place an American stamp on the
neo-colonial world then a-dawning. Not that Fanon – owing to his early
death – could easily have extended his analyis to predict the imperializing
world of multicentric global capitalist control that the problematic of
"recolonization" by a new "Empire of Capital" evokes in our day. And, in
any case, he was primarily preoccupied with grasping the precise meaning
of "independence" as defined not just by global capitalism but also by the
internal structures of those new "post-liberation" societies and states at
the periphery of the global capitalist system.

On this latter matter in particular his analysis was eloquent and
powerful:

> The national middle class discovers its historic mission: that of intermediary.
> Seen through its eyes, its mission has nothing to do with transforming the na-
> tion; it consists, prosaically, of being the transmission lines between the nation
> and a capitalism, rampant though camouflaged, which today puts on the masque
> of neo-colonalism. The national bourgeoisie will be quite content with the role of
> the Western bourgeoisie's business agent, and it will play its part without any com-
> plexes in a most dignified manner. But the same lucrative role, this cheap-jack's
> function, this meanness of outlook and this absence of all ambition symbolize the
> incapability of the national middle class to fulfil its historic role as a bourgeoisie.[15]

Not that this "national middle class" could (its ostensible "liberation"
of their countries to the contrary notwithstanding) readily have found the
requisite space vis-à-vis an immensely powerful and controlling western
capitalism to easily compete along national capitalist lines as any sort of
genuine bourgeoisie. In any case, it had no strong inclination to do so,
content as it was with "waving aloft" in its own interests "the notion of
the nationalization and Africanization of the ruling classes" and calling
that "liberation."[16] Such new elites would come, on Fanon's account, to
wield, as rentier elites and intermediaries for global capitalism, virtually
unchecked local power, brandishing the single party state and effective

---

15   Frantz Fanon, *The Wretched of the Earth* (Penguin Books: Harmondsworth, 1967),
        p. 122.

16   *Ibid.*, p. 125.

class dictatorship (even when there was, occasionally, more than one party allowed) in order to supervise the pacification of the people – feeding the latter only a diet of ethnic division and cruel overlordship, rather than encouraging them to have any sense of their own possible empowerment. In fact, Fanon's litany of the shortfalls, the "pitfalls," of the post-colonial African history was formidable and premised his grim and convincing interrogation of the colonial aftermath, one virtually unmatched by any analyst since.

Indeed, it was this preoccupation that made Fanon's seminal work *The Wretched of the Earth* a virtual bible of left thinking on the continent about such matters in the 1960s (as my own experience teaching in Tanzania [1965 to 1972] during the period showed me). For, even while celebrating the nationalist movements' victories, Fanon chose also to underscore the severe limits of such accomplishments. The achievement of state power primarily meant, as he chillingly demonstrated, the imposition upon the mass of the people, and despite their freshly awakened aspirations, of a new structure of domination. True, Fanon himself died in 1961, his *Wretched of the Earth* having been first published in French that same year. Thus, uncannily accurate as his analysis was, he was only drawing on a limited range of early cases of decolonization in Africa in establishing his paradigm. And yet his analysis – and his prescience – were so highly attuned to developments on the ground that the decolonizations of the 1960s played out along much the same lines that Fanon had extrapolated from his own direct experience in Africa in the 1950s.

Of course, Fanon did see other possibilities in which more funda-mental kinds of demands for real freedom were, as concrete practices of liberatory intent, taking shape. As he wrote,

> In the colonial countries where a real struggle for freedom has taken place, where the blood of the people has flowed and where the length of the period of armed struggle has favoured the backward surge of intellectuals towards bases grounded in the people, we can observe a genuine eradication of the superstructure built by these intellectuals from the bourgeois colonialist environment...Now it so happens that during the struggle for liberation, at the moment that the native intellectual

> comes into touch again with his people, this artificial sentinel [of presumed West-
> ern cultural superiority] is turned into dust.[17]

Perhaps he overestimated the extent to which this would prove to be the
case in Algeria, the revolutionary experience with which, in Africa, he
was most closely identified. Others, however, were tempted to see in the
liberation struggles launched, after Fanon's death, in southern Africa
similar seeds of fundamental change and the prospect of a new future
for Africa. To this sort of vision we will return.

But first note, in this respect, the complementary formulations of a
second gifted analyst of, and activist within, Africa's liberatory process,
Amilcar Cabral. For he too – writing in the 1960s – was sceptical as to "the
true nature of the national liberation struggle," wondering whether the
"national liberation struggle is not [in fact] an imperialist initiative"! For

> ...there is something wrong with the simple interpretation of the national libera-
> tion movement as a revolutionary trend. The objective of the imperialist countries
> was to prevent the enlargement of the socialist countries, to liberate the reaction-
> ary forces in our country which were being stifled by colonialism, and to enable
> these forces to ally themselves with the international bourgeoisie.[18]

Yet Cabral also glimpsed – both in his native Guinea-Bissau and more
generally – a possibly distinctive mode of African decolonization in play
in some settings (like Guinea-Bissau), one linked to armed struggle and a
more active mode of popular insurrection than colonial powers normally
permitted their colonies to experience.

The driving force of such a more revolutionary nationalism would
have to be, Cabral felt, a radicalized peasantry and working class.
Nonetheless, he acknowledged that an even more immediately critical
stratum is what he – his formulation here differing from, though parallel
to, Fanon's less exact notion of the "national middle class" – termed the
"petty-bourgeoisie." This he defined as "a stratum of people in the service
of imperialism who have learned how to manipulate the apparatus of the

---

17   *Ibid.*, p. 36.

18   This and the following quotations are from Amilcar Cabral, *Revolution in Guinea:
An African People's Struggle* (London: Stage 1, 1967), pp. 57–59.

state – the African petty bourgeoisie: this is the only stratum capable of controlling or even utilizing the instruments which the colonial state used against our people." As a result,

> ...we come to the conclusion that in colonial conditions it is the petty bourgeoisie which is the inheritor of state power (though I wish we could be wrong). The moment national liberation comes and the petty bourgeoisie take power we enter, or rather return to, history, and thus the internal contradictions break out [although] when that happens, and particularly as things are now, there will be powerful external contradictions conditioning the internal situation, and not just internal contradictions as before.

This meant that, on the one hand, the increased openness of the neo-colonial world actually increased the seductions offered to the emergent petty-bourgeoisie-in-power as, in particular, American firms began to enter into competition for economic control of colonies once more formally subordinated to Europe.

Yet, at the same time, Cabral also felt different outcomes to be quite conceivable. He therefore asked, quite straightforwardly, "What attitude can the petty bourgeoisie adopt?" answering that

> ...obviously people on the left will call for revolution; the right will call for the "non-revolution," i.e. a capitalist road or something like that. The petty bourgeoisie can either ally with imperialism and the reactionary strata in its own country to try and preserve itself as a petty bourgeoisie or ally itself with the workers and peasants who must themselves take power of control to make the revolution. We must be clear what we are asking the petty bourgeoisie to do. We are asking it to commit suicide. Because if there is a revolution, then the petty bourgeoisie will have to abandon power to the workers and peasants and cease to exist *qua* petty bourgeoisie.[19]

Can we really expect, however, that the leadership of a liberation struggle will act merely as a self-liquidating vanguard in the service of genuine popular struggle and in the interests of a genuinely popular-democratic outcome? Cabral reflected on the "character" of any such "revolutionary petty bourgeoisie" in the following terms:

---

19 As Cabral further remarks: "For a revolution to take place depends on the nature of the party (and its size), the character of the struggle that led up to liberation, whether there was an armed struggle, what the nature of this armed struggle was and how it developed and, of course, on the nature of the state" (*ibid*, p. 57).

> If I may put it this way, I think that one thing that can be said is this: the revolutionary petty bourgeoisie is honest; i.e., in spite of the hostile conditions, it remains identified with the fundamental interests of the popular masses. To do this it may have to commit suicide; by sacrificing itself it can reincarnate itself, but in the condition of workers and peasants. In speaking of honesty I am not trying to establish moral criteria for judging the role of the petty bourgeoisie when it is in power; what I mean by honesty, in a political context, is total commitment and total identification with the toiling masses.

In sum, Cabral believed that the experience of mobilization and commitment demanded by an armed and focussed liberation struggle against a recalcitrant colonial or white settler government could encourage its (almost-inevitably) petty bourgeois leadership to be "honest" in this way. Many felt the same kind of sustaining of revolutionary commitment was especially possible, even probable, in southern Africa where a similar kind of liberation struggle was already in train. Of course, Amilcar Cabral was assassinated by the Portuguese (and by traitors within his own movement) before he could witness that no such revolutionary and transformative outcome was to be forthcoming in Guinea-Bissau. But, *pace* Cabral, the same dispiriting denouement to "successful" struggle was to characterize southern Africa as well. To this sobering denouement to the region's liberation struggles we now turn.

3. South and Southern Africa: From Anti-Apartheid to Anti-Climax[20]

As examined in chapter 1 southern Africa has been a terrain upon which both the drama of anti-colonial struggle post-1945 and the shifting patterns of imperial rule have been clearly etched. For, unlike the situation of most of the other sites of liberation on the continent, a more dramatic confrontation with colonial powers – whether it be against an old-style colonial empire (like Portugal's) or against the authoritarian settler-colonial regimes left behind by colonialism (such as marked much of the

---

20   See also my "Globalization, Recolonization and the Paradox of Liberation in Southern Africa," ch. 15 in Arianna Lissoni, et. al. (eds.), *One Hundred Years of the ANC: Debating Liberation Histories Today* (Johannesburg: University of the Witwatersrand Press, 2012); and my "On Taming a Revolution: The South African Case," ch. 4, above.

rest of southern Africa) – would be required.[21] This in turn meant that anti-colonial action by local populations would have to be armed and/or rooted in particularly pronounced grassroots militancy if it were to succeed at all. In fact many of us who were politically active and alert in the 1960s and 1970s sensed – mistakenly as it turned out – that southern Africa might, in the long run and because of this, produce something very different from the earlier continental pattern so clearly identified and criticized by Fanon.

For one thing the white settler governments established in Rhodesia after its UDI and in Namibia and South Africa could not (unlike the British and the French further north in Africa) conceive and act upon any form of "false decolonization" – for they knew that any such outcome would throw their own domination on the ground as a privileged white elite into serious question. And Portugal, the one colonial power still directly active within the region, was not interested in false decolonization either, sensing that stronger imperial powers than itself would displace its influence if it attempted this in its colonies of Mozambique and Angola. Add to this the fact that, throughout the region, capital – especially in mining and related sectors, and both domestic and foreign-owned – had for an extended period been quite comfortable with the overall framework of racial rule. Capitalists were therefore quite willing to compromise over any relatively minor contradictions in the precise meshing and fine-tuning of racist and capitalist logics, accepting this in deference to their crucial interest in ensuring the supply of labour, cheap and pacified, that southern Africa's settler/apartheid rule had guaranteed.

On the other hand, the very intransigence of white-minority rule did tend to radicalize indigenous opposition to it as such opposition began to grope its way forward from the 1960s on. For it had become clear to aspi-

---

21 As regards Algeria, an earlier case where both French colonialism and a settler colonial presence were important and an armed struggle necessary, Fanon (*The Wretched of the Earth* [*op. cit.*], p. 154) emphasizes "the important part played by the war in leading [our own people] towards consciousness of themselves" – while also emphasizing the importance of the fact that "the work of clarification undertaken by a party [had] led people to the same result."

rant African nationalists throughout the region that some combination of armed struggle and/or high level of popular mobilization and action on the ground would be necessary in order to realize any significant progress. And indeed this radicalization of nationalism began increasingly to pose an ever greater threat to the status quo – threatening to bring revolutionary, even socialist, demands, not merely nationalist ones, front and centre. Of course, this also began to become particularly clear to the holders of capital, especially in South Africa itself – this country being much the highest stake for capital in the region. Indeed, in South Africa savvy capitalists would eventually become a major force for change, up to and including the abandonment of apartheid for something approximating to the (relatively) colour-blind rule of capital itself.[22]

Not that the "positive" implications of the requirement imposed upon the region's various nationalist-cum-liberation movements to actually organize to fight were entirely straightforward and self-evident.[23] After all, and more negatively, the apparent imperatives of "armed struggle" also reinforced various hierarchical and undemocratic pressures upon politics, pressures that further strengthened the realpolitik of tough, no-nonsense vanguardism – a politics that the "liberation movements" (and the governments they would eventually create) were also learning from both their autocratic hosts in the front-line African states bordering on the conflict zone itself, as well as from their Stalinist allies of the East. At the same time, so real a struggle for liberation did imply the need to mobilize people to a more committed level of involvement than was true in a situation where the nationalist leadership would, in the end and as Fanon had predicted, merely be ushered into power by the departing colonialists.

Nationalist leaderships could change of course – could begin "to commit suicide" – as certainly happened promisingly (albeit momentarily) in Mozambique. And in South Africa the actual motor-force of effective

---

22　Saul, "On Taming a Revolution," *op. cit.*, and chapter 4, above.

23　*Pace* Fanon's chapter 1 ("Concerning Violence") in *The Wretched of the Earth* (*op. cit.*).

confrontation was less an armed liberation movement (the ANC) than the rising tide of assertion at workplaces and township: in Durban and Soweto in the 1970s, and ever more generally as the wave of resistance crested in the 1980s. Thus, even if – as many of us at the time feared might prove to be the case – the ANC balked at ensuring an ever more expansive practice of liberation in the post-apartheid period, its feet could, in effect, be held to the fire of revolutionary purpose and democratic practice by the popular energies unleashed by the nature of anti-apartheid struggle itself. In so arguing, I don't think those of us who glimpsed such a possibility were merely – or even mainly – being naïve. Instead, we were being hopeful.[24]

But unrealistic nonetheless, as events were to prove.[25] For the sober fact remains that the leadership of the southern African liberation movements proved, to an alarming degree, to be perfectly comfortable with the general pattern marked out by previous continental decolonization – and perfectly prepared to defend their own growing stake in it. After all, as elsewhere, such leaderships were comprised primarily of a would-be "national middle-class" (Fanon): aspirant *men* (emphasis added) on the make, prepared to face up to the somewhat harsher path to power that intransigent white hierarchies forced upon them but in the end quite willing to conform (in pursuit of their own nascent class interests) to the global status quo. For the latter's "logic" closed in on them insistently, crystallized both in the seductions and the pressures of global capitalist power wielders from state and corporations alike. And there was also the parallel temptation of subservience towards an established local hierarchy, especially (as in the South African case) towards the central position of white entrepreneurs – at least when the hierarchy of local class power was

---

24   Indeed, demobilizing any such counterforce became an important focus of ANC political practice both during the transition to formal democracy and after; on this see my essay "On Taming a Revolution: The South African Case" (ch. 4, above).

25   On this subject see the various articles, one of each of the five sites of actual liberation struggle in the region, in the special themed section on "Southern Africa: The Liberation Struggle Continues," in *Review of African Political Economy (ROAPE)*, #127 (March, 2011), pp. 77–134, including my own introduction to this section. See also my "Class, Race, Gender and Voice (*op. cit*).

so modified as to remove race as the major barrier to the new black elite's own entry into such circles! In short, as Colin Leys and I argued some years ago, "dependency" remained the most accurate description of these countries' immediately visible fate. And given the difficulties in Africa, as elsewhere, of crafting and implementing alternative socio-economic strategies, it seemed, perhaps, easier

> ...to be driven back to a reformist position, hoping at best to shift the existing arrangements and rules marginally in favour of the countries of the South, to give them some room for manouevre within the existing global capitalist system. Yet [as we argued], in Africa no convincing case has been made for a genuinely developmental alternative to socialism as a response to dependency.[26]

So, despite the fact of having experienced militant, even armed, struggle there, the Fanonist paradigm had come to hold as true for southern African countries as it had for countries further to the north in Africa. For those Africans in power in southern Africa were now to serve merely as a service-elite facilitating the exercise of the economic power of what was primarily externally-based capital, thus becoming the region's very own exemplification of Fanon's "intermediary" class. The sub-continent was, in sum, to remain largely subordinate to global capitalist requirements in its political-economic profile, as, primarily, a source of raw materials and of oil (Angola) and a range of mineral resources. Small wonder that one is still tempted, as stated above, to describe southern Africa in terms of a continuing pattern of unqualified subordination – even if its subordination is to a more diverse range of corporate global masters/corporations than had been the case for earlier African colonies on the continent as they had also "freed" themselves from formal colonialism.

In fact, to the widespread and fundamentally non-developmental dependency in Africa – now widely viewed as the apparent fate of so many countries there – there are, in theory, only two possible alternatives.

---

26 Colin Leys and John S. Saul, "Dependency" in David A. Clark (ed.), *The Elgar Companion to Development Studies* (Cheltenham: Edward Elgar, 2005) and also our "Sub-Saharan Africa in Global Capitalism" in *Monthly Review: Special Summer Issue on Global Capitalism*, July–August 1999.

(a) One such hypothesized alternative is to follow a presumed capitalist route to "development," one driven by a more locally-centred (though internationally viable) and vibrant capitalist productive process that would begin to produce more wealth (for elite consumption in the first instance but, with a promise of trickle-down advantages for the broader population), or...

(b) A second, quite different alternative would be a socialist one, a system that, through imagination and planning, would be both more broadly productive and more open to the claims of equitable distribution and democratic action from below than any capitalism in Africa (whether dependent or more assertively economically independent) could be expected to be.

As for, on the one hand, a possible capitalist route forward, this is the position, derived from a particularly unremitting reading of Marx, that Bill Warren once made prominent regarding the developmental prospects of the "Global South": "imperialism" as "pioneer of capitalism" (with any movement towards socialism "correctly" to be delayed until capitalism had done the necessary dirty work of accumulation and the formation of a revolutionary proletariat). Indeed, given the new diversity of capitalist intruders in Africa (beyond the usual suspects from the great white global north-west), this may seem to some (including the dominant elites in some African countries) a more likely prospect for them than ever: providing an opening up of space for such elites, now as fledgling capitalists themselves and not merely as gatekeepers for global corporations in their countries. In some such way Joe Hanlon (as seen in chapter 3, above) hints at a new path for Mozambique (its socialist project launched immediately after independence having "failed"). And he nominates the country's president (Armando Guebuza), his family and his political-cum-business cronies for some such bold new role as "national bourgeoisie."[27]

---

27 For a sharply critical perspective on Hanlon's position, but with numerous footnotes pointing the readers towards Hanlon's own presentation of the position, see my "Mozambique – not then but now" in the ROAPE collection cited in footnote 22, and, as chapter 3, above.

Jesse Ovadia apparently harbours similar hopes for Angola (and for Nigeria),[28] having clearly listened closely to the claims of that country's dominant elite. He highlights, in his own analyses, the latter's aspirations for capitalist success – and the possible transformation of their own countries along such lines. Indeed, he sees the substantial oil revenues of Angola (and also of Nigeria) as less the "resource curse" that some observers have defined them to be; for him, they ensure a platform for Angola and Nigeria's promising "petro-developmental states" (as he labels them[29]), providing the financial basis for the further (and potentially quite transformative) entrepreneurial activities of these countries' elites. To be sure, any such transformative effects are still more rhetorical in nature than as yet realized in practice. For, in truth, much of what both Hanlon and Ovadia actually single out as earnests of successful domestic capitalism seem primarily to still represent a sub-stratum of subordinate (and relatively untransformative) entrepreneurial activities that are merely complementary to the more significant undertakings of much more important global players. In fact the jury must still be considered as being out, under African conditions, on the efficacy of, and the lofty promises for, what Ovadia terms "petro-developmentalism" (or of something similar that might happen elsewhere).

In fact, the same sceptical questions are posed in South Africa as well where a key element of the ANC's policy package is nothing less than a self-described "Black Economic Empowerment" programme. Interestingly, however, Moeletsi Mbeki, brother of South Africa's former president, Thabo Mbeki (who was himself an early mover of BEE), has said that most of the apparent "empowerment" of black entrepreneurs transpiring in his country has been, precisely, a kind of sham empowerment of a service-cum-tenderpreneurial class – with he himself calling instead for efforts to support a much more meaningful, creative and productive national

---

28   See Jesse Ovadia, "The Reinvention of Elite Accumulation in Angola: Emergent Capitalism in a Rentier Economy," *Cadernos de Estudos Africanos*. Vol. 25 (Jan–June 2013).

29   Indeed, one wag has, in turn, termed Ovadia's position as exemplifying "petro-Warrenism."

bourgeoisie than anything yet seen.[30] Indeed, Moeletsi seems to be saying, regretfully (since he would consider himself a presumptive claimant to a role within any such rising South African national bourgeoisie[31]) that dependency still rules and that any local capitalism still has a long way to go before it can hope to emulate some of the successes of its presumed counterparts in Korea, China and India.

But what, as an alternative, of building socialism? There are, of course, many southern Africans who would agree with Moeletsi Mbeki as to the thinness of claims for a genuinely transformative capitalist solution along the lines (dependency plus BEE!) presently pursued in South Africa and elsewhere in the region. But some would disagree with him forcefully as to the likelihood of realizing any more liberating option within some different, more Afro-centric and more nationally expansive, capitalist framework. Instead these are those who continue to champion the possibility of a quite different path to the future: a socialist path. For them, the promise of socialism is not only that it would seek to realize a much more equitable, democratic and just Africa but also that it would produce, by thoughtful planning, a far more productive one.[32]

True, building socialism – and finding traction in alternative terms to those otherwise dictated by global capitalism in a predominantly capitalist world – is certain to be difficult, as unlikely, perhaps, as realizing a genuinely developmental capitalist way forward (although certainly not any more so).[33] Moreover, previous efforts to ensure a socialism that is truly controlled by the people in whose name it claims to be acting has

30   See Moeletsi Mbeki, "Wealth creation: Only a matter of time before the hand grenade explodes," *Business Day* (Feb. 10, 2011).

31   We will, however, return, to Moeletsi Mbeki's preoccupations in this Conclusion and at greater length, below.

32   For an example of one possible such assertion, see Democratic Left Front/DLF, *1st Democratic Left Conference Report* (Killarney, SA: 2011) and also Vishwas Satgar and Mazibuko Jara, "New times require new democratic left," *Mail and Guardian* On-line, Feb 7, 2011.

33   On this claim, more generally, see John S. Saul, "Is Socialism Still an Alternative?" (*op. cit.*).

already proven to be no small task – as the experience of both Tanzania and Mozambique (chs. 2 and 3, above) in the first years after independence/liberation attests. Indeed any hopes that Cabral might once have had for the full expression of popular power and of equity in the wake of, quite specifically, "liberation struggle" have been bruised and not only by the continuing strength of global capitalism. For the proclaimed imperatives of vanguardism and claims to personal privilege have come to characterize the "victorious" southern Africa elites – those who have, quite simply, refused to "commit suicide" in any meaningful Cabralian sense.

4. Recolonization...and Renewed Resistance

In sum: in southern Africa Cabral's hope that freedom, especially when it had been won under the most difficult of colonial circumstances and by the most militant of possible means, might actually give rise to continuing popular benefits in the form of meaningful liberation from the material ignominies of the past has not been realized. The liberation first claimed by African states that came to their apparent freedom from formal colonialism proved very quickly to define them as mere neo-colonized prisoners of a world dominated by American empire. True, there did come to exist in the early twenty-first century, a more open and competitive global capitalism, one with multiple centres of capitalist power. But the questions spawned by such a reality must be faced squarely. Does such a world of capitalism really provide greater space for African countries to better, competitively, their economic prospects? Can their elites in power now realistically fancy themselves as entrepreneurial and national capitalist players in their own right (rather than as the merely state-cozened wards, rentiers, and well-paid intermediaries of global capitalism that their predecessor national elites have been)? Or do severe limits not continue to exist as to how far Africa and its elites can advance, competitively, along any such path? In short, does the world of capital, however freshly variegated it may now be (with Brazil a formidable player in Mozambique for example and China asserting the same role throughout the region), not still structure Mozambique – in its underdevelopment and "historical backwardness" – as a dependent actor vis-à-vis international capital? Have we not witnessed, in fact, a virtual recolonization of liberated southern Africa – recolonization by what can only be termed an "Empire of Capital"?

At the same time, in Africa the accomplishments of self-proclaimed progressive, even socialist, elites have not so far been very effective in delivering on their offers to the marginalized African people of real respite from the enormous costs of an over-bearing global capitalism. But if Africa cannot really hope to find liberation either from continuing dependency or from the will-of-the-wisp of a liberatory indigenous capitalism, what does it in fact need? The not so simple answer: it needs new sources of hope, clear-thinking and inspiration – one, two, many Cabrals! – in order to conceive and to craft more popularly-driven, democratically effective and economically progressive and egalitarian programmes and movements to deliver on the promise of previous notions of southern African "liberation." For the fact is that the governments of all five of the "liberated" countries of southern Africa still float on the misleading bubble of the triumphant anti-colonial nationalism of an earlier era. But this is a nationalism that can now be seen clearly to be exhausted and to have failed – and no amount of petty entrepreneurial bluster or of any too glib scholarly romanticism of right or left can easily change the terms of the continent's dependency that dictate its relative marginalization.

Fortunately, of course, there do remain radical ideas afoot in the region, especially in South Africa, as well as radical energy from below to be tapped and focussed. Consider, again, South Africa and note, once again, that the much discussed "rebellion of the poor there" has placed the country at the very top of the world table as regards the occurrence of incidents of social unrest and local resistance.[34] But how can radical theory and practice now move forward (in South Africa this now also must be

34   See Peter Alexander, "Rebellion of the poor: South Africa's service delivery protests – a preliminary analysis," *Review of African Political Economy*, v. 37, #123 (March, 2010) as well as his updated survey entitled, "SA protest rates increasingly competitive with world leader China," 23 March 2012, available at http://www.amandlapublishers.co.za.

done in the wake, notably, of the horrors of a massacre at Marikana that has so graphically illustrated the cruel contradictions of the country's present system[35])? Here, then, is a very big question to put on the agenda in the following section.

B. The New Struggle: On Liberating Liberation in South Africa[36]

There are some political stirrings from the left in southern Africa, in Mozambique and elsewhere, although the truth of the matter is that even in the Mozambican case these, as Pitcher alludes to them, are still more fledgling and attitudinal than firmly organizational and meaningfully ideological in nature. And beyond Mozambique, in Angola and Namibia, such signs of political hope for a next liberation struggle are even more notional and evanescent than that. As for Zimbabwe any promise that the MDC might once have been thought to offer there has largely evaporated, stymied, quite literally, by the state's willful violence and the serial refusal of Mugabe and company to accept popular electoral rejection; in consequence there has tended to be the slow wearing away on the stony ground of SADC indifference and internal political machinations of the MDC's principles and of its effective progressive practice.[37]

---

35   See on this question (with reference to the South African case) Peter Alexander, Thapelo Lekgowa, Botsang Mmope, Luke Sinwell and Bongani Xezwi, *Marikana: A View from the Mountain and a Case to Answer* (Johannesburg, Jacana, 2012. and John S. Saul and Patrick Bond, *South Africa – The Present as History* (*op. cit.*), especially chs. 5 and 6.

36   An earlier (and since much reworked) version of this section (B) of my conclusion was first presented, under the title "Mounting a New Counter-Hegemonic Project in Contemporary South Africa: Moeletsi Mbeki, Zwelinzima Vavi and the Democratic Left Forum," at a session on "From Human Rights to Counter-Hegemony," at the Annual General Meeting of the Canadian Association of African Studies (CAAS) held at York University, May 6, 2011 and under a similar title, at the Socialist Register "Workshop on Socialist Strategy Today" at the Sociology Department, Puck Building, New York University, May 14, 2011.

37   Various authors, "Theme: Southern Africa – the liberation struggle continues," 2011. *Review of African Political Economy/ROAPE*, #127, pp. 77–134.

Indeed, in southern Africa each of the movements that delivered independence in the decades before 1994 remains ever more determined to cling (successfully, as each of them has) to power and to reject both any meaningful popular empowerment from below and any broad-gauged development effort that might service mass needs and demands. This has offered an extremely grim outcome to the years of liberation struggle in fact, one grimly parallel to the prognosis as to the nature of "liberation" that we have seen Frantz Fanon to suggest to be the fate of the first continental struggles for independence from formal colonialism further to the north in Africa during the 1950s and 1960s. For this pattern has now proven to be equally true for southern Africa.[38]

And yet it is in South Africa itself that one can see the glimmerings of some signs of a revival of the struggle for equity, justice and meaningful liberation as well. In concluding this volume I will highlight some such signs here, deploying somewhat more extensively than is my normal authorial custom the actual texts of South African observers and actors in order to make the invoking of their voices that much more tangible and real for the reader.

1. "The rebellion of the poor"

The first clue to what is beginning to happen in South Africa is that provided by the wide range of popular protests recorded by Peter Alexander and others in recent writings. Indeed, the weight and significance of such protests – summarized so clearly by Alexander – seem indicative of a growing social distemper, one ripe, precisely, for the further stimulus of counter-hegemonic ideology and effective organizational initiatives. Thus, in an evocative article in ROAPE on what he terms the current "rebellion of the poor," he writes (as quoted at greater length in the previous chapter): "Since 2004 South Africa has experienced a movement of local protests amounting to a rebellion of the poor. This has been widespread and intense, reaching insurrectionary proportions in some cases." And he concludes that "while the inter-connections between the local protests, and

---

38   See, again, Ch. 4, above.

between the local protests and militant action involving other elements of civil society, are limited, it is suggested that this is likely to change."[39]

Nor has this surge from below since died down, as Alexander clearly demonstrates in a more recent article:[40]

> In 2010/11 there was a record number of crowd management incidents (unrest and peaceful), and the final data for 2011/12 are likely to show an even higher figure. Already, the number of gatherings involving unrest was higher in 2011/12 than any previous year. During the last three years, 2009–12, there has been an average of 2.9 unrest incidents per day. This is an increase of 40 percent over the average of 2.1 unrest incidents per day recorded for 2004–09. The statistics show that what has been called the Rebellion of the Poor has intensified over the past three years.

As he continues:

> The main conclusion we draw from the latest police statistics is that the number of service delivery protests continues unabated. Government attempts to improve service delivery have not been sufficient to assuage the frustration and anger of poor people in South Africa. From press reports and our own research it is clear that while service delivery demands provide the principal focus for unrest incidents, many other issues are being raised, notably lack of jobs. As many commentators and activists now accept, service delivery protests are part of a broader Rebellion of the Poor. This rebellion is massive. I have not yet found any other country where there is a similar level of ongoing urban unrest. South Africa can reasonably be described as the "protest capital of the world." It also has the highest levels of inequality and unemployment of any major country, and it is not unreasonable to assume that the rebellion is, to a large degree, a consequence of these phenomena. There is no basis for assuming that the rebellion will subside unless the government is far more effective in channelling resources towards the poor.

True, all this has still been happening within the frame of continued ANC national electoral dominance – even though the ANC does tend to sustain its continuing large percentage of the vote (even if from the increasingly diminishing number of those amongst the population who actually exercise the franchise at all!) In fact, popular unease seems thus

39   Peter Alexander, "Rebellion of the poor: South Africa's service delivery protests – a preliminary analysis," *Review of African Political Economy*, v. 37, #123 (March, 2010).

40   Peter Alexander, "SA protest rates increasingly competitive with world leader China," *Amandla! Online*, 23 March 2012, available at http://www.amandlapublishers.co.za.

far to find its chief expression most assertively at the local level, with the ANC still granted primacy as the presumptive god-father of liberation at the national level. Nonetheless, there have also been other signs that the ANC's hegemony may have begun to fray – and certainly few among the citizenry seem to strongly harbour the belief that the ANC offers developmental answers that will positively affect the quality of their own lives. But breaking definitively the commonsense of ANC rule and establishing a credible, viable, counter-hegemonic challenge to its rule remains an elusive goal.

We will have to examine this increasingly difficult situation briefly below, although we will have to do so with great care and caution. Still, it is the case that the kind of rebellious energy recorded by Alexander has already found, from time to time, expression that seemed to carry some such genuinely counter-hegemonic promise. For example, in 2002 I felt myself to be witness to such promise when I participated in the dramatic march from Alexandra to Sandton of many thousands of civil society activists to protest the World Summit on Social Development the ANC was then hosting.[41] And I have also sensed similar energies afoot on other occasions, at the workshop of the Municipal Services Project in Cape Town in 2007 for example, where again I participated with a large group of representatives from various township groups straining to articulate a broader vision.[42] Was a wave of dissent building that might come, effectively, to challenge the grim realities of South Africa's present? This was not yet quite the case, unfortunately. But what of the present moment? Let us first examine other voices to get some greater sense of the kinds of rumblings that are beginning to be heard.

2. Moeletsi Mbeki and the North African Moment

For, in this respect, a second clue as to the likely future seems to have been provided, as we have alluded to earlier, by Moeletsi Mbeki, one-time

---

41 The "moment" of the Alexandra-Sandton march is discussed in my "Starting from Scratch: A Debate," being ch. 10 in Saul, *The Next Liberation Struggle* (*op. cit.*).

42 Saul, "The Strange Death of Liberated Southern Africa" in *Decolonization and Empire* (*op. cit.*).

leftist and gad-fly in exile from South Africa during the struggle years, brother of former president Thabo Mbeki (and son of ANC/SACP patri- arch Govan Mbeki) and now a rising entrepreneur in a post-apartheid and firmly capitalist South Africa. Moreover, his is no doubt a "clue" more rhetorical than real – important more as a fresh current of thought from a somewhat unexpected source of skepticism as to the future of the starkly unequal society that South Africa remains. But the cues that have stimulated his intervention have been real enough: not only the signal distemper of contemporary South Africa sketched above but also the mass popular expressions of anger and discontent against self-serving govern- ments that have marked Tunisia and Egypt in recent years. It is, of course, far too early to assess what the medium and long-term implications are in either of the latter cases (although the further signs are not nearly as promising as one might have hoped). Nonetheless, the intrinsic drama and apparent potential of the "Arab Spring" has been felt throughout the continent – including in South Africa and certainly by Moeletsi Mbeki.

For Mbeki draws – in a dramatic, outspoken and very public way – a clear parallel between South Africa and such continental precedents. Not that Moeletsi is any stranger to controversy. During the liberation struggle he always set himself (as I remember him from Dar es Salaam days in the 1960s) at some distance from the ANC and later, as a journalist and commentator, he often took a position overtly and even ostentatiously to the left of the ANC's official line. Nor did he ride into office, either political or administrative, with the transition to ANC hegemony. Instead, despite the fact that he did, from time to time, keep a line of leftist chat going, he also moved skillfully with the tide of Black Economic Empowerment to consolidate his role as a successful black entrepreneur in the new, post-apartheid South Africa. For example, I can myself clearly remem- ber him launching, at a private University of Witwatersrand dinner, an extremely strong attack, from a black entrepreneurial standpoint, both on the very limited vision of the official "Black Economic Empowerment/ BEE" initiative itself and on his brother's own subservience to global capi- tal – interpreted by Moeletsi to be at the expense of a more meaningful empowerment of local private interests (a theme he has reverted to, as we shall see, in his sensational Tunisia intervention, discussed below, a decade later!). A man of the left gone right, then, when the South African opportunity offered itself. But enough of a leftist to not allow himself to be easily fooled about what was actually happening in the country. Hence the importance of his Tunisia statement:

> I can predict when SA's "Tunisia Day" will arrive. Tunisia Day is when the masses rise against the powers that be, as happened recently in Tunisia. The year will be 2020, give or take a couple of years. The year 2020 is when China estimates that its current minerals-intensive industrialization phase will be concluded.

> For SA, this will mean the African National Congress (ANC) government will have to cut back on social grants, which it uses to placate the black poor and to get their votes. China's current industrialization phase [having momentarily] forced up the prices of SA's minerals, which has enabled the government to finance social welfare programmes.

> The ANC inherited a flawed, complex society it barely understood; its tinkerings with it are turning it into an explosive cocktail. The ANC leaders are like a group of children playing with a hand grenade. One day one of them will figure out how to pull out the pin and everyone will be killed.[43]

Mbeki's provides his own set of indices, beyond his predicted end of the windfall from China's minerals-grab strategy, of this situation: the fact that life expectancy has declined from 65 years to 53 years since the ANC came to power and that, in 2007, the country became a net food importer for the first time in its history; that the elimination of agricultural subsidies by the government led to the loss of 600,000 farm workers' jobs and the eviction from the commercial farming sector of about 2.4 million people between 1997 and 2007; and that "the ANC stopped controlling the borders, leading to a flood of poor people into SA, which has led to conflicts between SA's poor and foreign African migrants."

The ANC's central policy pillar, Mbeki continues forcefully, has been one of "protecting SA's conglomerates"? And yet there are, in his view, "many things wrong with how conglomerates operate and how they have

---

43 The quotations from Moeletsi Mbeki in this sub-section of the chapter are drawn from Mbeki (*op. cit.*).

structured our economy." These "many things" he then itemizes as follows: "The economy has a strong built-in dependence on cheap labour; it has a strong built-in dependence on the exploitation of primary resources; it is strongly unfavourable to the development of skills in our general population; it has a strong bias towards importing technology and economic solutions; and it promotes inequality between citizens by creating a large, marginalised underclass." A strong indictment indeed.

The rest of his speech was, as suggested, something of a reiteration of Moeletsi's table talk at Wits a decade earlier, with a conclusion as to what instead is "the correct road SA should be travelling" – albeit now with even more skepticism concerning the role played by the rather parasitic, tag-along, form of Black Economic Empowerment that has in fact been sponsored for ANC cronies and patronized by the conglomerates under that label. In Mbeki's words, "My quarrel with BEE is that what the conglomerates are doing is developing a new culture in SA – not a culture of entrepreneurship, but an entitlement culture, whereby black people who want to go into business think that they should acquire assets free, and that somebody is there to make them rich, rather than that they should build enterprises from the ground." For "we cannot build black companies if what black entrepreneurs look forward to is the distribution of already existing assets from the conglomerates in return for becoming lobbyists for the conglomerates." No, Mbeki wants a much more serious form of development of a "national bourgeoisie" to be put in place. As he concludes,

> We all accept that a socialist model, along the lines of the Soviet Union, is not workable for SA today. The creation of a state-owned economy is not a formula that is an option for SA or for many parts of the world… [I]f we want to develop SA instead of shuffling pre-existing wealth, we have to create new entrepreneurs, and we need to support existing entrepreneurs to diversify into new economic sectors.

In sum, for Mbeki, only a vibrant national bourgeoisie can hope to stave off a South African "Tunisia" in 2020.

> Nothing new, then, from Mbeki. Nonetheless, the aggressively public nature of this intervention (in the widely-read South African newspaper *Business Day*), the continentally-charged linking of his position with the bogey of current Tunisian

events and the shade of his recently disgraced brother Thabo unfairly laid at his doorstep by subsequent commentators lent his remarks real saliency. For it proved that he had stirred up a hornets' nest – with banner newspaper headlines very soon announcing that "ANC rejects Mbeki's 'Tunisia Day' claim: 'ANC says SA's fledgling constitutional democracy cannot be equated with tyranny or stagnation in the country's growing economy'"![44]

Indeed the opening paragraph of one of the articles to be found under such headlines juxtaposed two events with apparently intended irony, reading: "The African National Congress (ANC) yesterday disputed predictions by political analyst Moeletsi Mbeki that the South African government would face a Tunisia-style revolt, on the same day that police fired live ammunition to disperse residents who took to the streets over poor service delivery in Mpumalanga" – adding that "Municipal IQ, a Johannesburg-based company that researches local government trends, said public service protests were increasingly becoming a tool used by citizens disappointed with government performance. Last year saw a record number of marches as citizens sought a way of being heard. The protests were growing into a 'socio political phenomenon,' with 111 recorded across municipalities last year, according to Municipal IQ. There were 105 recorded in 2009, while there were 10 in 2004 when monitoring of the protests began."

Nonetheless, as the article continued,

ANC spokesman Brian Sokutu yesterday hit back at Mr Mbeki's claims. "Our fledgling constitutional democracy, which continues to make inroads in redressing decades of apartheid, cannot be equated with tyranny or stagnation in our growing economy, as Moeletsi insinuates." SA had a stable democracy, with a number of bodies that supported it, like the Office of the Public Protector and the Human Rights Commission, Mr Sokutu said.

Mr Mbeki merely retorted, the article then stated, "that 'people don't eat democracy'!"[45]

---

44 Simon Mkokeli, "ANC rejects Mbeki's Tunisia Day claim," *Business Day* (February 16, 2011), p. 3.

45 See, for a number of these quotations, Mkokeli, *ibid.* As for the generally rather more intemperate ANC Youth League, the *Citizen* (February 18, 2011) reported its official spokesperson Floyd Shivambu as labelling Mbeki's prediction one of "the

The explicit response to Moeletsi Mbeki by South Africa's president Jabob Zuma was also of interest: thus Zuma said that he was

> ...confident that South Africa will never become "a second Tunisia". Zuma gave this assurance in an interview with *Beeld* [a South African newspaper]on Wednesday, amid violent protests about poor service delivery and unemployment in Mpumalanga and North West. He fervently rejected predictions that South Africa was heading towards a situation similar to that in Tunisia...firmly disagreeing with Mbeki from his office in Tuynhuys, while television footage of the Ermelo protest marches flashed in the background. "I don't want to become personal, because it is not in my nature. But it is easy to be clever, to sit back and to criticise," he said.[46]

Zuma explained there were fundamental differences between the governing circumstances in South Africa and Tunisia. According to him there were no parallels between the history, politics and social conditions of the two countries. "How and on which basis do you compare apples and guavas? That is how it is with analysts: They analyse and criticise without doing the work or giving alternatives."[47]

3. Zwelinzima Vavi and the Civil Society Trope

Unlike Mbeki, Zwelinzima Vavi, head of COSATU, is far from advocating...indigenous entrepreneur. Instead, he provides a third clue to the

---

most bizarre to ever happen," adding that Mbeki was living on a "different planet" in "day-dreaming that the people of South Africa will revolt to topple the ANC government inspired by his hatred of the African National Congress." He then laid the (unlikely) charge that Mr. Mbeki has become "very pessimistic and consistently negative about the progress made by the ANC government, particularly since the departure of his brother as president"!

46   L. Steenkamp and P. du Toit, "SA won't be a 2nd Tunisia – Zuma," *Beeld* (February 7, 2011).

47   Mbeki responded to Zuma in *News24*, 2001, "Moeletsi Mbeki confronts Zuma on slight," *News24* (February 29, 2011): [R]eacting to an interview in the *Beeld* newspaper last week, where Zuma described him as being among the intellectuals who criticise the government rather than contribute to building South Africa, "Mbeki was sufficiently annoyed to say that he was 'stung by being dismissed by Zuma and believed the slight was related to the bad blood between the president and the man he succeeded as ANC leader...I think he's trying to fight his battle with my brother through me,' he said." All the more so, wrote Moeletsi, in light of a private meeting he and Zuma had had not long before in which Zuma had responded far more positively to his comments.

South African puzzle by seeking to speak out forthrightly in the name of workers' interests – and increasingly for those speaking from within an even broader civil society. In doing so, he has, in recent years, provided ever more expansive signals of nascent but articulate dissent. This was most notable in November, 2010, when a new initiative by Vavi and COSATU (much the largest trade union central in the country) reached out quite independently to strengthen its links with actors in civil society and, notably, with organizations representing "the poor."

For even though it remains tightly bound to its alliance with the ANC and the SACP (the Tri-partite Alliance) COSATU has seemed to chafe from time to time at the ANC overall policy of unqualified neo-liberal subservience to capital. The combination of the ANC's sometimes quite outspoken and menacing threats to labour's existing status within the Alliance alongside just enough labour-friendly legislation to remain marginally credible as an ally, has been enough to date to keep the union – despite its occasional dramatic and oppositional mass demonstrations with regard to various issues – hewing to the party's line. But what does such schizophrenic solidarity/subservience actually mean in broader terms? Does this reflect well-calculated and intelligent caution on CO-SATU's part? Or is it actually, as some would argue, more a continued pursuit of the advantages held by the bulk of the unions' members (to be found at the upper end of the hierarchy of urban workers and township dwellers) in much the same way that Lenin had once suspected an earlier Western European "labour aristocracy" to be acting. When I spoke on a panel at a 2002 Canadian Labour Congress working session alongside Vavi, he expressed a certain cagey awareness as to the potential ambiguities inherent in COSATU's close relationship in the alliance with a government like that of South Africa, ambiguities that I sought to specify in my own contribution to that discussion as follows:

> There are not [yet] many people saying that the alliance should be smashed and a new left party built. It would not be an easy thing to do. However, as Comrade Vavi has just pointed out there are many more people [now] saying that it is time to figure out a way to hold the ANC's feet to the fire and that the unions alone cannot do it, because they are going to be dismissed as just another special group. Instead

it is necessary to build a movement...of all the groups [in civil society] and to begin together to become more effective players.[48]

Could concerned observers now hope, a decade later, for something more from Vavi, some further steps towards the forging of an effective working relationship between "proletariat" and "precariat" than COSATU had, in the post-apartheid epoch, hitherto sought to achieve?

Further, was some kind of answer to this question to be seen when Vavi's COSATU in late-2010 took the above-mentioned step of reaching out to "civil society" at the conference – specifically held without ANC or SACP official involvement – with representatives from a wide range of activist civic organizations (both those more and those less close to the ANC itself)? For Vavi appeared himself to be arguing forcefully an apparently quasi-dissident line:[49] "Inspired by the African proverb that says 'If you want to go quickly, go alone. If you want to go far, go together,' we gather here – as the progressive trade unions, social movements, NGOs, progressive academics, small business and street vendor associations, taxi associations, religious bodies, youth organizations, environmental groups, indigenous peoples' groups and other progressive formations – to say to ourselves that we have the capacity to make a decisive contribution in changing our current situation for the better." As he continued:

> The global governance, commercial and trade system is supported by political and ideological institutions, rules and enforcement mechanisms that only broad civil society coalitions have historically been able to challenge successfully.[50]

---

48   In Paul Leduc Browne (ed.), *Labour and Social Democracy: International Perspectives* (Ottawa: Canadian Centre for Policy Alternatives, 2011): 61–70.

49   See Zwelinzima Vavi, October 28, 2010. See also Bukezela Phakathi, "COSATU launches UDF to Rescue Country," *Business Day* (October 28, 2010), in which he writes: "Warning that SA faced a 'national catastrophe,' COSATU yesterday launched a major civil society effort to tackle corruption, poverty and unemployment. COSATU General Secretary Zwelinzima Vavi, in his address to the Civil Society Conference, evoked the landmark formation of the anti-apartheid United Democratic Front in 1983, but was at pains to stress that his was 'not an anti-African National Congress and anti-government coalition: The challenge we face today...we saw in those years,' Mr Vavi told the delegates at the launch in Boksberg."

50   These he here specified as follows: "Internationally, globalization and neoliberal-

In South Africa, the GEAR strategy epitomised the dominance of the neoliberal ideology within the leading sections of the government. The neoliberal logic still continues to be dominant, in spite of some talk about a developmental state. Increasingly though it has taken a more crude political expression and there are some emerging elements that tend to perceive the working class and active elements of civil society as merely being a nuisance that must be crushed with the might of the state apparatus.

Today, as we gather here, there is panic in the ranks of the predatory elite, which is a new coalition of the tenderpreneurs. Paranoia elsewhere is deepening with the political elite convincing itself that any gathering of independent civil society formations to confront our challenges is a threat to them.

Of course, Vavi was quick to assure his audience, especially the audience beyond the hall where his speech was being delivered, that "we are not an anti-ANC and anti-government coalition. We are not here to begin a process to form any political party, nor to advance the interest of any individual. We have only one enemy – neoliberalism that has condemned our people to poverty and unemployment. We want to roll back neoliberal advances and struggle for the adoption and implementation of alternatives." But the fact remains that the ANC had long since pledged its unqualified allegiance to neoliberalism and, in any case, even his above-quoted demurrer could not save Vavi from instant and quite predictable attack. For if Moeletsi Mbeki, as gadfly, could stir up a hornet's nest of ANC criticism, this was as nothing compared to the angry response Vavi provoked as head of COSATU, ostensibly one of the ANC's closest allies and pillar of the governing Tri-Partite Alliance. Certainly, it appeared, the "political elite" did feel threatened! As Mandy Rossouw's attendant story was headlined in the *Mail and Guardian*: "COSATU conference 'pains' ANC: Ruling party incensed that alliance partner is 'ganging up' with NGOS." As she continued,

In an uncharacteristically emotional response the ANC accused COSATU of following Zimbabwe's Movement for Democratic Change [the opposition group in that country whose initial impetus came from the trade unions] and rejected the

---

ism have launched assaults on the working class, which include, but are not limited to: informalization, flexibilization, regionalization of states, deregulation, marketization, financialization, and securitization"!

trade union federation's plea that the conference was not about cementing opposition to the ruling party.[51]

For the ANC had continued its counter-attack, its Secretary General Gwede Mantashe going so far as to state that "the conference had positioned itself 'as an alternative bloc to the [ruling] alliance.'" While "it's not an opposition party, the stance is oppositionist. It is a dangerous populist approach to disagreements, and it is intending to create a crisis where there is no crisis...We caution that an action [like this] one of leading a charge for the formation...of a mass civic movement outside the alliance and the ANC might indeed be interpreted as initial steps for regime change in South Africa." This overheated response to the conference came despite the fact that, as the story continues, there had been "temporary cease-fire between the ANC and COSATU [that] emerged after the ANC's national general council in September, [this itself coming] after months of tension over the country's economic trajectory and the ANC's perceived soft stance against corruption."[52]

Indeed, Rossouw found a second ANC spokesperson, Jackson Mtembu, who also "echoed this heated reaction," albeit in a more folksy idiom: "If you have a friend and that friend goes out and finds a bloc that mobilizes against you, how would you feel? We're speaking from the heart here. Our pain comes from this ganging up against the ANC leadership." As Rousouw further noted, "the ANC is also irked that conference delegates called government policies 'neoliberal' – the same term used to damn the policies of former president Thabo Mbeki." Mthembu also took issue with Vavi's "reference at the conference to a 'predatory elite' in the ANC. 'If you don't name names, you're saying it's all of us,' he said."

Finally, the same article by Rousouw stated that COSATU president Sdumo Dlamini was in turn "taken aback by the ANC's harsh response

---

51   Mandy Rossouw, "COSATU conference 'pains' ANC," *Mail and Guardian* (November 5 to 11, 2010); Mthembu (below) is also quoted from this article. See also Rossouw, "2011 may be the year that civil society rises as an opposition force," *Business Day* (January 6, 2011).

52   Mwantashe's attack is quoted in "ANC leadership paranoid – Vavi," *News24* (February 3, 2011).

to the conference." And the union's more formal rejoinder was also soon forthcoming:

> The ANC leadership was paranoid in interpreting a civil society conference as an attempt to effect regime change in South Africa, COSATU general secretary Zwelinzima Vavi told the SABC on Tuesday. "I honestly don't know what informs this paranoia on the part of the leadership. COSATU went with the overwhelming majority of the people who attended...It was very clear that we were not going there to form a workers' party or a new left wing party or whatever."[53]

True, the ANC itself immediately denied that it was being paranoid, Mantsashe responding that "the issue is that the ANC has a relationship with COSATU. Therefore if you are going to flirt with other people, you talk to your alliance partners, so that there are no suspicions." As he added, "there [are] 'living examples' of civil society organizations being funded to oppose liberation movements, for example Zimbabwe's Movement for Democratic Change [sic]. Reality informs our perceptions, not paranoia." For some "civil society organizations [are] hostile towards the ANC and the issue was that its alliance partner had 'flirted' with these groups," Mantashe said.[54]

In response, COSATU spokesperson Patrick Craven chose merely to reinforce the union's original point, himself expressing "shock" at what he felt to be the ANC's over-reaction: "The [ANC] statement fails to understand the nature and role of civil society in the national democratic revolution and raises totally groundless fears of the formation of an opposition bloc," he said, and then continued as follows:

> "COSATU remains firmly committed to its alliance with the ANC, SACP and Sanco, mandated by many national congress resolutions. It has however always been, and will remain, a trade union federation, independent of the ANC, the state and capital, with the right to meet and interact with any organization, as long as it advances the interests of the working class." COSATU does not need to seek permission from anyone to meet and work with friendly pro-poor and pro-working class organizations, Craven said.[55]

---

53 As also quoted by *News24*, *ibid*.

54 As quoted in *News24* (November 4, 2010), "COSATU conference: ANC leadership not paranoid."

55 As quoted in *ibid*.

Righteous anger? A retreat? Or did it suggest that where there's smoke there's fire and, in effect, promise more of the same kind of boldness? Only time will tell, although Vavi himself would return to the charge only a few months later, in February 2011. For the chief topic of his address to the South African Conference of Bishops' Justice and Peace Conference turned on the fact that "clearly we do not live in a society where everyone is happily living in peace. And the underlying reason is the continuation of poverty and inequality. Which brings me to my topic tonight – the poor." As he then stated: "We have a constitution which grants people certain rights. Yet in practice millions are denied those rights, especially socio-economic rights, in what has become the most unequal nation in the world." Thus, "the rich elite earn millions by exploiting the labour of the working class. A minority, including some of our former comrades in public office, make their millions by corruptly manipulating opportunities to win tenders, bribing officials or using political connections." Meanwhile,

> the mainly black poor majority suffer from deep and widespread poverty, huge levels of unemployment, pathetic levels of service delivery in healthcare and education, housing and transport, and little hope of escaping from a life of struggling to survive from day to day. We are one of the most unequal countries in the world, and unless we mobilize for changes, the levels of inequality will become entrenched.[56]

And again, later in the year, in a COSATU central committee report,[57] Vavi made very similar arguments. Small wonder that Mandy Rossouw could headline one of her articles: "2011 may be the year that civil society

---

56   In this keynote address (Vavi, 2011) Vavi then further specified, "There is no official poverty line for South Africa, yet even the Minister of Finance has acknowledged that 50% of the population lives on 8% of national income in South Africa. In 1995, the Gini coefficient, which measures inequality, stood at 0.64 but had increased to 0.68 in 2008. The workers' share of income was 56% in 1995 but by 2009 it has declined to 51%.On the other hand the number of South African billionaires nearly doubled, from 16 in 2009 to 31 in 2010 and the country's 20 richest men enjoyed a 45% increase in wealth."

57   S. Ngalwa, and A. Majavu, *Times Live* (June 12, 2011), "Vavi stuns ANC: COSATU general secretary Zwelinzima Vavi warns in a report prepared for the federation's central committee meeting this month that South Africa could become a 'banana republic,' and threatens to repudiate President Jacob Zuma's leadership."

rises as an opposition force."[58] And even if this did not quite happen in 2011 there were, in fact, others who saw the years ahead to be even more promising in this respect.

4. The Democratic Left Forum/DLF: Harbinger of a New Politics?

Of course, one earnest of the latter prospect comes from the evidence of a "rebellion of the poor" in South Africa recorded by Peter Alexander and cited above. But a final clue comes from evidence that suggests the forces constituting "civil society" might be beginning to find a counter-hegemonic voice – and ever more effective organizational and assertively political expression.[59] No doubt many who foresee such a possibility would like to see it also linked to a more independent trade union/COSATU presence – with the unions slipping further away from their often subordinate position within the AACP/SACP nexus and moving to help realize a much more promising proletariat-precariat oppositional alliance/movement. The politics of such possibilities are still fledgling ones at best, it must be admitted. Nonetheless, to get some further fix on what any such new politics might be beginning to entail, I will take the Democratic Left Front as exemplifying the sort of present initiative that, in one form or another, will have to take further root if a necessary and truly burgeoning counter-hegemonic left-political presence is ever to be realized.

But first: what about the possibility of some such fresh, progressive and necessary initiative arising instead from within the ANC/SACP camp itself? We have seen some indication of just this in my concluding paragraph to chapter 4 (above) with citation of the provocative report by Canadian correspondent Geoffrey York headlined "ANC's radical voices growing louder: Proposed agenda includes black economic ownership, farm expropriation, nationalization and tighter controls on the courts."[60]

---

58   Mandy Rossouw, "2011 may be the year that civil society rises as an opposition force," *Business Day*, January 6, 2011.

59   "Zwelinzima Vavi's keynote address to the SACBC Justice and Peace AGM," CO-SATU Press Release (Feb. 26, 2011).

60   Geoffrey York, "ANC's radical voices growing louder," *The Globe and Mail* (Toronto, 8 June, 2012).

And further indication of this could be found in the debate around the much-discussed notion of "a second transition" at the ANC's policy conference at the end of June, 2012. Unfortunately, most media observers and many participants found this primarily to be so much sound and fury signifying very little.[61] Indeed, in a trenchant piece critiquing the "second transition" theme (designed as it was to lay out guidelines for carrying the thrust of constitutional struggle more forthrightly into the realm of the economy), Jeremy Cronin suggests that the agenda for any such transition would have to be much bolder. For both the document and the debate suffered from an

> inability to clearly analyse the systemic nature of our challenges [that] leads to a tendency in the document to portray the economic growth path we inherited (what the document describes as an "apartheid colonial" economy) as essentially characterized by "white ownership" of the "major means of production". This can easily lead to the assumption that de-racialising ownership will change the system and the trajectory of our "developmental" path. Clearly our economy was racialised (and remains racialised in many respects), but the document tends to be silent about the more deep-seated features of our "apartheid colonial" economy – excessive unbeneficiated export dependence, excessive dependence on capital imports, incredibly high levels of monopoly concentration and particularly the dominance of the mining-finance oligopolies and the historic weaknesses of the manufacturing and small enterprise sector, a dualistic labour market, etc.[62]

Yet such crucial questions as the latter are ones that the ANC has shown no real taste for grappling with. Nor is it likely soon to develop any such propensity, one fears.

No, the posing of questions and the suggestion of answers will have to come from elsewhere, from others distinctly less sanguine about pinning hope on one wing or another of the ANC/SACP, but instead seeing both as too compromised by their entanglement in the recolonization process to offer much hope of genuine creativity. Can, for example, the

61 Patrick Bond (ed.), July 4, 2012. "ANC Policy Conference reactions," as distributed to the DEBATE-list (debate-list@fahamu.org).

62 Jeremy Cronin, "The 'second transition': let's not get sucker-punched into a false debate," Amandla!, at http://www.amandlapublishers.co.za/special-features (July 22, 2012) and Vishwas Satgar, 'The ANC's Second Transition: Another Dead-End?" At http://www.amandlapublishers.co.za/special-features (July 22, 2012).

"Tunisia" potential of South African society, as unequal and hierarchical as it has become, be encouraged to express itself in an independent and even more organized, principled and self-consciously left fashion than either Moeletsi Mbeki (as, now, from the centre-right of the political spectrum) would dare conceive or Zwelinzima Vavi (from the centre-left) be inclined to countenance.

Vavi's COSATU/civil society pow-wow certainly did represent the momentary promise of bigger legions and clearer principles. Nonetheless, rightly or wrongly and whatever the future may bring, Vavi is most reluctant to break with the Tripartite Alliance and take union-civil society links to a new level of independent political action. Yet, as suggested, there are those in South Africa who are prepared to pronounce even more forcefully their commitment to the necessary prospect of a more coordinated, programmatic and independent left possibility at the heart of South Africa society – a project-in-the-making that, they feel, has found expression in the numerous outbursts of labour militancy and the impressive range of township and rural outrage and protest that have been going off like firecrackers across the country in recent years. And that may well be encouraged to speak out with a more unified, militant and counter-hegemonic voice.

Small wonder, then, that in a context that can produce such assertions as Moeletsi Mbeki's "leftish" posturing on behalf of a more empowered "national bourgeoisie" and Vavi's tantalizing outreach to civil society, others should now be moved to think even more boldly. Hence, to return to this sub-section's primary focus: the conference held January 20–23, 2011 that led to the establishment of a new and promising Democratic Left Front (DLF). The National Covening Committee of this conference (composed of Mazibuko Jara, Brain Ashley, Jane Duncan, Ayand Kota, Trevor Ngwane, Phumi Mtetwa, Martin Legassick, Noor Nieftagodien, Alan Murphy and Vishwas Satgar) made this quite clear in their "Foreword" to the impressive 84 page document, entitled "Another South Africa and World is Possible: 1st Democratic Left Conference Report (UDF, 2012)" – a document that summarized the conference's discussions and outcomes and set out the premises for the kind of innovative collective action they had in mind. As it made its case there,

> Post-apartheid South Africa is experiencing a social crisis due to neoliberal global-ization. The old apartheid pattern of development has continued with a few elites (and now Black elites) benefiting while the majority are enduring profound suf-fering. Deepening poverty, inequality, hunger, homelessness, unemployment and ecological destruction are affecting the working class and the poor the most. We believe this has to be confronted to ensure our post apartheid democracy works for all. Moreover, we refuse to accept that the workers and the poor of South Africa need to carry the cost for the current global crisis that has come to our shores. At the same time, the organizations of the working class and the poor have been weakened, divided and have generally found themselves in a state of desperation. An effective transformative politics advancing anti-capitalist alternatives for the country has not been able to come to the fore. This represents a strategic defeat for the South African anti-capitalist left as a whole.[63]

As the document then continued, "Through the 1st Conference of the Democratic Left…we are making a call to the workers, the poor and the anti-capitalist left to draw the line and to fight back. Our conference was an important milestone in a long journey to regroup anti-capitalist forces and to reclaim lost ground." Promising, but note here again the centrality of the formulation: "the working class and the poor," a very self-conscious linkage that parallels, as we have noted, our linking in this volume of the concepts of "proletariat" and "precariat."[64] It is a formulation that holds much promise for the kind of expansive radicalism envisioned. Moreover, another central theme, much emphasized, was "democracy," this being emphasized at least as often as class action. Though some of the apparent cadres of this DLF had indisputably vanguardist backgrounds this was not the kind of thrust to be found in their document or in their most clearly articulated public statements.

Business Day sought to tease out the implications of the DLF's launch, asking whether here was "the seed of a new opposition?" – and sub-titling their article "How long the tripartite alliance will survive has been the sub-

---

63   Democratic Left Front, *Another South Africa and World is Possible: 1st Democratic Left Conference Report*, 20–23 January 2011, University of Witwatersrand, South Africa, 80 pages: photocopy (2001).

64   See ch. 5, above.

ject of debate for almost as long as the African National Congress (ANC) has been in power." This article concludes with an interesting comment on the DLF, described it as an assemblage of "left-leaning social movements, civil society groups and nongovernmental organizations" and suggesting that "the similarities between the DLF and the former UDF will surely not go unnoticed by the ANC. The organizers are all former activists and unionists, and many participated in the controversial civil society conference that was convened last year and attended by COSATU" (although COSATU, the article acknowledges, was not a founding organization of the DLF and was not officially represented at the launch). And it concludes that "even though the front does not [yet] see itself as a political party and has resolved not to participate in this year's local government elections," it is also the case that "judging from the number of former ANC and SACP stalwarts in its ranks, and the similarities between their concerns and those now being openly acknowledged by senior members of the ANC, this is a space that should be watched carefully in the next few years."[65]

Similarly, in *Pambazuka News* (January 27, 2001), Mphutlane wa Bofelo wrote that the new DLF, established "by social movements, community organizations, political parties, labour unions and working-class organizations across the ideological spectrum of anti-capitalist left politics, is the most positive development in the efforts to creatively and proactively deal with the challenges presented by the neo-apartheid, neoliberal capitalist dispensation."

> The DLF is envisaged to be a mass political movement that seeks to explore and establish bottom-up, people-driven participatory democratic forms of organization and people's power beyond elections, the government, the state and the party-political space. Therefore the DLF does not obsess with state power nor does it seek to transform itself into a political party contesting elections. Its focus is connecting and escalating the struggles of the poor and working-class communities and exploring and building together with communities – through action and the culture of "each-one-teach-one" – sustainable, democratic, and egalitarian, eco-friendly economies and community driven development.[66]

---

65   "The Seeds of a New Opposition," *Business Day* (February 7, 2011).

66   Mphutlane wa Bofelo (*Pambazuka News*, January 27, 2011).

Interestingly, much was heard of the precedent of the old United Democratic Front in the anti-apartheid struggle days. Interestingly, too, the DLF has held open its door to an eventual, more overt, trade union presence, even scheduling its own launch event so as not to give any impression of seeking to conflict with some parallel COSATU public activity on those dates.

It remains to be seen what the new organization will seek to do in coming months in order to sustain and expand both its visibility and its credibility, of course. Certainly, the overall tenor of self-presentation was sober. Various of my own correspondents close to the process acknowledged that it was "very early days yet." Another, while stressing that the participants were "mostly African" and that "potentially there is a huge base for the DLF in civil society [in] the massive protests that characterise SA," conceded that "at present DLF is relatively small – 250 delegates at the conference representing perhaps a few thousand people."

Nonetheless, two of its principle organizers, Mazibuko Jara and Vishwas Satgar, spoke out strongly, convincingly and promisingly in a *Mail and Guardian* article pegged to the DLF launch:

> Our conference is merely a milestone in a long journey that has to do with trying to reimagine a left politics through ethical practice. Our ethical compass is about living and inventing democracy inside this process (definitely through heated debates, differences and new ways of thinking about consensus), plurality as strength, collective intellectual practice, self-education and building transformative power through struggles.
>
> This is a process without preconceived outcomes and thus is unique in South Africa. Such a process means abandoning the illusions of a vanguardist left committed to a violent overthrow of capitalism or a reformist left seeking to make capitalism more humane.
>
> More importantly, we are about strengthening and advancing grassroots struggles through opposition but, at the same time, advancing transformative alternatives from below.
>
> This is illustrated by the ideas, proposals and campaigns that were adopted as part of our common platform of action dealing with ecological resources, unemployment, food sovereignty, education and public services.[67]

---

67 Vishwas Satgar, and Mazibuko Jara, "New times require new democratic left." *Mail*

In short, here were signs of a new movement afoot in South Africa which, if not yet providing any firm answer to the country's ills, does demonstrate that there are South Africans who are taking the challenges that face them very seriously indeed. In fact, as suggested earlier, I have chosen to record the views of South Africans on this issue, and in their own voices, as extensively as I have in this concluding chapter precisely to give a better, more concrete, sense not only of the "rebellion of the poor" (the scope of which Peter Alexander has captured so well in his recent essays) but also of the counter-hegemonic sensibilities that demonstrate the willingness of many South Africans to think through how best to consolidate the present "rebellion" into an effective alternative project.

C. What Next?

To conclude: what now?, and what next? In principle the regional future is open but this is deemed to be true by various activists and authors in two quite distinct and sharply definable ways. On the one hand, it is hypothesized that the situation throughout the sub-continent will, for the foreseeable future, continue to be locked within an overall frame of global capitalist hegemony (read, I have argued, "recolonization"). On the other hand, something quite different, something much more socialist, could instead be imagined as possibly emerging as a viable alternative.

Take the first prognosis first, while also noting that the overall framework of increased subordination to global-capital's socio-economic hegemony does actually offer several sub-sets of conceived possibilities. One of these prognoses takes quite seriously a quasi-Warrenite paradigm, hypothesizing a capitalist way forward towards some sort of economic and social "development." Recall, in this regard, the instructive title of Warren's most celebrated publication *Imperialism: Pioneer of Capitalism*. For, even though a prophet of global capitalist development, Warren remained Marxist enough to hypothesize, in the ripeness of time and with the further flowering of capitalism, some eventual prospect of a "genuinely" proletarian revolution and grounded socialist possibility. Many others

and Guardian On-line (Feb 7, 2011).

who share the same analysis and who similarly embrace the economics of imperialism (if not the socio-political carapace of direct "colonial domination" that so often served to frame it) have no need of such an attendant hypothesis to their enthusiasm for capitalism, however: they merely take the prospect of a developmental capitalist option seriously without having any attendant long-term socialist prospect in mind.

True, such analysts often do paint, at least for public consumption, a relatively benign and prosperous outcome, one with perhaps some fairly grim inequality in its immediate workings but one that can be predicted to be, in the end, beneficial to all in these peripheral capitalist societies as they inch their way up the global ladder. Along some such lines their forerunners in more advanced capitalist regions of the world are said to have stayed poverty and many forms of social distemper (after the manner of the saying "a rising tide floats all boats"). Now, quite simply, it is our turn, the yea-sayers claim: such is the broader rationale behind the ANC's policies in South Africa and such a prospect is one that we have seen observers like Hanlon and Ovadia to hold out for countries like Mozambique and Angola as well.

Nonetheless, in their franker moments, many of the local beneficiaries of the real and existing capitalisms that mark Africa are content merely to be quite comfortable in their own personal and class "success" and privilege as they preside over capitalisms that are nonetheless "failed" as developmental projects – projects that have become stalled in deepening inequality and in the political marginalization of the poor which is now so evident throughout southern Africa. This should not be too surprising an outcome. After all, it has been one of the staples of progressive thinking about development over many years that, quite simply, the global spread of capitalism does not draw all territories that the system touches forward but is in fact sharply polarizing of the world in its implications. In sum, many poor countries, not least in Africa, simply cannot easily compete with the countries that are further "ahead" in the capitalist race and, without a dramatic shift in the premises of their socio-economic practice, are doomed to deepening "underdevelopment."

Indeed, the truth is also that if things in Africa don't get better for the vast majority of the population along such capitalist lines they can, quite predictably, be expected to get much worse. This is true not only with respect to the yawning gap between rich and poor, though it is this gap, in particular, that underpins the resort to high-handed authoritarianism throughout the continent (most dramatically, within our region, in Zimbabwe and Angola perhaps but elsewhere as well). Or, if not a distinct pull towards overt authoritarianism, there is a strong drift on the part of the new elite towards a sustained indifference to, and demobilization of, the broader populace, these latter left in so many ways to rot in underemployment and penury. Nor are these latter the only distempers characteristic of presently existing southern Africa: under such circumstances individualistic solutions to the challenges of people's frustrated lives can readily facilitate a turn to murder, rape and robbery – or, if more collectively felt, they can be no more positive: xenophobia, ethnic violence and religious sectarianism, for example.

Small wonder that there remains an alternative, more progressive, kind of pull towards collective and progressive social purpose. This once found its chief expression in militant engagement against racial dictatorship in southern Africa and, briefly, in several expressions of continued struggle for socialist and more profoundly democratic outcomes as manifesting a logical sustaining of the commitment to a full and more meaningful liberation. As we have seen there are inklings of a rebirth of an ongoing "next liberation struggle" elsewhere in the region, but this is most impressively the case in South Africa – as we have indicated above. Indeed, the events of 2012 at Marikana may come to be viewed as a particularly significant milestone in the eventual depassing of the bleak aftermath of failed liberation in that country. Thus, as long-time ANC activist Pallo Jordan commented in Marikana's wake:

> Does it sit easily with the millions of ANC supporters here at home, and in the world at large, that during [the organization's] centennial year, the government, led by the ANC, presided over the first post-democracy state massacre...[For] Marikana is symptomatic of a much deeper malaise...Over the past eight years we have seen the escalation of local protests over perceived delivery failures and corruption

at local government levels. It might well be that many of these protests were fuelled by rising expectations: [Certainly] there can be no doubt that in many instances this has led to ANC councilors losing legitimacy among the people. It is only a matter of time before that loss of legitimacy percolates upwards – to the provincial and national levels...[Indeed] the credibility of the ANC today is probably the lowest it has been since 1990![68]

But, as we have seen, Jordan's is merely one of several interventions by movement worthies that could be cited here.[69]

Clearly, the situation in South Africa remains deeply troubling – although, from a longer term perspective, it may perhaps be deemed to be somewhat promising. Thus the efforts of such initiatives as that exemplified by the Democratic Left Front persist, the cracks between the ANC and COSATU also continue, promisingly, to deepen in the wake of Marikana, and an ever wider range of voices of concern as to the fate of a "free" South Africa are heard. We shall just have to see. Here, I will merely reiterate the words of my good South African friend Neville Alexander who, shortly before his recent death, stated of the present moment that

> The working and unemployed masses are voting with their feet. Whatever their lingering loyalties and ever more feeble hopes in the myth that "the ANC will deliver", however big the gap between political consciousness and material practice, the thousands of township uprisings, countrywide strikes and serial metropolitan protest actions have one simple meaning: we reject your policies and your practices as anti-worker and anti-poor. It is, in my view, a misnomer to refer to these stirrings of self-organization of the working class as an expression of "collective insubordination", even though their immediate impulse is usually reactive rather than proactive. They are saying very clearly and very loudly that the appeal to nationalist, blood and soil rhetoric has lost its power and that we are standing on the threshold of a politics that will be shaped by a heightened sense of class struggle.[70]

---

68   I quote from a copy of a speech to 20th commemoration of the commemoration at Bisho of the massacre there in 1992 and sent to me by Jordan himself on September 9, 2012.

69   I have included a number of these related quotations in my aforementioned conclusion to the recent history of South Africa that I have co-authored with Patrick Bond (*South Africa – The Present as History* [*op. cit.*]). Here, I will merely urge any reader who finds the present volume to be of interest to investigate that one as well.

70   Neville Alexander, "South Africa: An Unfinished Revolution?" This was the fourth Strini Moodley Annual Memorial Lecture, held at the University of KwaZulu-Natal on May 13, 2010 and, posted at *Links International Journal of Socialist Renewal*.

And so say an increasing number of us – relatively optimistically.[71]

Can the same kind of guarded optimism hold for the rest of the region? For, as we have suggested, the future there provides just as troubling a prospect – and an even less promising one. At the same time, however, recall as well that at the dawn of the 1960s the promise of any kind of liberation from the cancerous white minority rule of the time seemed equally bleak to those who took humane justice and basic human rights seriously – although not bleak to those smugly ensconced in positions of global power. Indeed, amongst the latter and as late as the early 1970s, Henry Kissinger and the American State Department could quite comfortably summarize the "facts" of the regional situation – their description offering to them at once both a best-case scenario and also what they claimed to be the one most likely to be true – as follows: "The whites are here to stay and the only way that constructive change can come about is through them. There is no hope for the blacks to gain the political rights they seek through violence, which will only lead to chaos and increased opportunities for the communists...Our tangible interests form a basis for our contacts in the region, and these can be maintained at an acceptable political cost."[72] Yet "white power" was not in fact to quite so straightforwardly triumph (even if many imperial interests were indeed to be "maintained") – thanks to the militant struggles of so many around the world and principally by those in southern Africa itself. Such warriors for freedom did not throw up their hands in despair at that dark time. There is no need for their successors to do so now.

---

71 As noted, for further reflection on the prospects for a radical post-Marikana politics see the separate conclusions drawn by Patrick Bond (ch. 6: "Uneven and Combined Resistance: Marikana and The Trail to 'Tunisia Day,'" 2020) and myself (ch. 7: "Liberating Liberation: The Struggle Against Recolonization in South Africa") in our aforementioned *South Africa – The Present as History: From Mrs. Ples to Mandela and Marikana* (Oxford: James Currey, 2014).

72 *The Kissinger Study of Southern Africa* (London: Spokesman Books, 1975), p. 66, this book being principally comprised of the response by the U.S. National Security Interdepartmental Group for Africa to the "National Security Study Memorandum #39: Southern Africa," and published with a useful "Introduction" by Barry Cohen and Mohamed A. El-Khawas.

"More Comfortably Without Her?"
Ruth First as Writer and Activist

I made the following remarks in June 2012 at the University of London's Institute of Commonwealth Studies to a symposium in honour of Ruth First, both to mark the thirtieth anniversary of her assassination at the hands of the apartheid state and to celebrate the launch of a project in London to digitize and preserve her collected papers. Thanking Leo Zeilig and his team at the ICS for their work in putting such an important symposium together and also Gillian Slovo, Ruth's daughter, for her presence there as a speaker that day, I then greeted others in the audience, many of them my old friends and comrades whom I was particularly pleased to see. Indeed, as I then said, this would have been quite a glorious occasion – if our thoughts were not at the same time so bitter and painful. I next presented my own contribution in London by looking backwards, to my own return to Canada shortly after her murder in 1982.

1. Ruth's Death and Our Memories

For I received, almost at once, an invitation to present a eulogy to Ruth First at the American African Studies Association's annual meeting. A difficult task but an appropriate occasion. The setting: Washington's Capitol Hilton Hotel, just down the road from Reagan's White House and in a vast ballroom which only minutes before had seen Chester Crocker, the administration's senior Africa-hand, flabbily rationalizing the United States' kid-gloves treatment of apartheid South Africa to another panel session of the same ASA meeting. Now I had the rostrum to say something of the other side of that struggle. And Ruth's friend Oliver Tambo, president of the African National Congress, the pre-eminent force for positive change in that country, was to follow me to first speak briefly of Ruth, but then, eloquently, of the present state of his movement's struggle against white-minority rule and racial capitalism. As I said on that occasion, Tambo's very presence

> reminded us of Ruth First's own role in the front ranks of that revolutionary struggle since the 1940s: as an editor (with such important publications, ultimately banned, as *The Guardian* and *Fighting Talk*), as a writer, as a political organizer, and as a mobilizer of the freedom struggle both within and without South Africa.[1]

As I was certain that Comrade Tambo would have something more to say on this score, I proceeded to speak of a second important dimension of her work, that being

> her intellectual contribution not only to the Southern African revolution but also to raising the intellectual and moral level of our own discourse. Consider, among many other writings, her early exposé of South Africa's role in Namibia (*South-West Africa*, 1963), her harrowing personal account of her own period of solitary confinement in a South African jail (*117 Days*, 1965), her revelations, with her co-authors, as to *The South African Connection* (1972) with western capitalism, her landmark study of militarism in independent Africa (*The Barrel of a Gun*, 1970) her recent blending of socialist and feminist perspectives in the biography of Olive Schreiner which she co-authored (*Olive Schreiner*, 1980).

But, I continued, there was of course one further aspect of her career, its most recent phase – a phase that produced, among other things, her book on Mozambique, *Black Gold* – and it was also one that I could speak about most confidently and at first hand: this was

> her role at the University of Eduardo Mondlane in Mozambique where, friends for some years previously, we became colleagues. Indeed, in the end, I was two minutes late for a farewell party which she had arranged in my honour, and in those two minutes, in her office in the Centre of African Studies, she died, opening a parcel-bomb, at South Africa's hand.

---

1   My speech, from which a number of the following quotes are drawn was incorporated, in part, in my "Laying Ghosts to Rest: Ruth First and South Africa's War." *This Magazine*, 17, 5, (December, 1983).

I then underscored the importance of Ruth's Maputo years, and their broader significance – but, as I said at the London colloquium, we had a whole panel of her co-workers there with us to do just that and I therefore wouldn't repeat that particular exercise. What I could say, however, was that the last years of her involvement in the southern African struggle spent participating in the attempt to build socialism in Mozambique very much paralleled her involvement in the continuing struggle for South African freedom – though, of course, she would have made no such distinction between the two struggles.

In this regard it continues to bear emphasizing that Ruth First was a brilliant social scientist – albeit a revolutionary social scientist (and, again, she would have made no real distinction between the two, between her roles as revolutionary and as social scientist). For, as a social scientist, she knew that there was no substitute for clear thinking and hard work – for a genuine science. And she knew that solidly-grounded revolutionary endeavour required and demanded no less.

Finally, in drawing my Washington speech to a close, I struck a more personal note:

> I doubt that there is anyone who knew Ruth First well who didn't have difficult moments with her. She was tough, demanding, even occasionally domineering. She was forged in a hard school, a revolutionary socialist and a woman fighting consistently and unflaggingly against racism, chauvinism and capitalist exploitation in the teeth of one of the most brutal regimes the world has ever seen and, fortunately for us all, she was ready to fight back for what she believed in.

> Besides, even when one looked back at moments of inter-personal tension one had had with her it was also with the realization that such tensions were not arbitrary ones, that almost invariably something important, intellectually and politically, was at stake. The seriousness of her engagement, the intensity of her concern, could never be doubted. Nor, if you were struggling to be as serious yourself, could such moments cast any doubt upon her personal concern, her compassion, her continuing solidarity in the next round of whatever struggle, public or personal, was in train.

> Now [as I then wrote] almost two months have passed since that August day in Maputo and, strangely, I still hear, from time to time, her voice echoing quite clearly and tangibly in my ears, snatches of earlier conversations and the like. I know this reflects the strength and continuing impact of her vibrant and powerful personality.

Perhaps others here will have experienced this as well and, of course, for each of us who hears it this will be a private voice. Yet, knowing Ruth, we need not doubt that it is also a political voice, a voice exhorting all of us, here and elsewhere, as "Africanists," as scientists, as activists, to continue the struggle for which she gave her life.

And I concluded a journal article of the time, one that included both my above-quoted speech and a recounting of my own return to Maputo a year after the assassination on a closely related and equally sobering note:

Laying to rest Ruth's ghost on my recent visit to Mozambique was, in fact, a prosaic enough moment. I had had to leave Maputo only days after the assassination and before the funeral. Now I was walking down the hall to Ruth's office where I sat so often in the past but had last seen only from the road as a gaping hole in the outer wall of the building. Not surprisingly, I found it humming with activity, the room itself now serving as the office of the centre's secretariat. How to avoid cliché: life goes on, the struggle continues. I thought of the five people whom I had known well in both political and personal contexts in Africa who had fallen to the assassin: Ruth; Eduardo Mondlane, Frelimo's first president (killed in 1969 in Dar es Salaam, where I was living at the time, by a book bomb sent by the Portuguese); Walter Rodney the Guyanese historian and activist who had been my next-door neighbour for many years in Tanzania, assassinated in his native Guyana after leaving the continent; Samora Machel, killed in the downing of an airplane drawn off course (it now seems clear) and to its destruction by the South African state; and Aquino de Bragança, victim of the same crash who was also injured in the room when Ruth herself died. Was I, was the movement, "stronger at the broken places" in the wake of such horrors? Probably not. But, of course, there is no real alternative but to act as if we are, to get on with it. We owe such comrades at least that much.[2]

Her work as scholar-activist

In his own book on Ruth and her writings Don Pinnock took the pains to search out for citation in his book the article of mine referred to above, one otherwise buried in the pages of a magazine I edited in Canada many years ago. Let me return the compliment by referencing an important book of his, part biography, part a selection of major writings by Ruth from over the years. In it, he speaks particularly eloquently on the topic

2   *Ibid.*

several of us sought to address on the panel at the aforementioned London symposium: "Ruth First, the Writer and Activist," and I quote:

> Ruth's involvement in the 1946 mine workers' strike, followed by her farmworker exposés, focussed her writing on the struggle between capital, labour and the State in a way no other journalists of the period were doing. She was therefore best placed to see the implications in the plethora of legislation and regulation which followed the 1948 election and to understand the baggage of labour legislation that the new government has inherited from the old. For Ruth it was not the individuals or the parliamentary Acts that made history, but the context which made them possible...[Of course], she wanted to know how institutions worked, who they were composed of, where the power lay, who benefited from them and how that impacted on individuals. [But] she also wanted to break them open to public scrutiny and action.[3]

Like Berthold Brecht before her, Ruth wrote (Pinnock himself concludes) to provoke her readers to action and also to "discredit the legitimacy of the existing regime." For as Brecht himself once put it in his powerful poem "To Posterity":

> For we went, changing our country more often than our shoes,
> In the class war, despairing,
> When there was only injustice and resistance.

But Brecht, like Ruth, did not really "despair," both continuing to offer resistance of their own. As Brecht continues,

> There was little I could do. But my rulers
> Would have slept more comfortably without me.
> This was my hope.[4]

Slept more comfortably without Ruth? This is what Craig Williamson and the other killers and terrorists who populated the South African state apparatus (right to its very apex) must have hoped for when they moved so brutally to still her voice in August thirty years ago.

---

3   Don Pinnock, *Voices of Liberation: Ruth First* (New Edition), (Cape Town: HSRC Press, 2012), pp. 26–7.

4   Bertolt Brecht, "To Posterity" in *Selected Poems* (New York, Grove Press, 1959), pp. 174–176.

What might she have said?

I needn't dwell on the loss: all of us who are in London today, I then said, must certainly feel it. But I will mention one particular place where her loss particularly gnaws at me. We learn, for example, from Gillian's book, *Every Secret Thing*, that Ruth quarreled with Joe about the implications of the Soviet intervention in Czechoslovakia which she condemned.[5] For she always had something challenging to say. So, I can't help asking myself, just what would Ruth have said, more contemporaneously, about what liberation has come to mean in South Africa – a result that I myself have characterized in recent writing as having seen the country, in effect, "recolonized" by a still dominant Empire of Capital. I did then note that I had written an article on this topic for next year's *Socialist Register* [now also chapter 4 of this book, above] and, in any case, I had come to celebrate Ruth and not myself. Much more appropriate, I thought, to evoke the close-to-final thoughts on post-apartheid developments of a dear friend of Ruth's who outlived her by several decades, a stalwart comrade, Rusty Bernstein. I summon his voice from a letter [already quoted from several times above in the present volume] he wrote to me shortly before his death in 2002, a letter that contained the following words:

> The drive towards power has corrupted the political equation in various ways. In the late 1980s, when popular resistance revived again inside the country led by the UDF, it led the ANC to see the UDF as an undesirable factor in the struggle for power, and to fatally undermine it as a rival focus for mass mobilization. It has undermined the ANC's adherence to the path of mass resistance as a way to liberation, and substituted instead a reliance on manipulation of the levers of administrative power. It has paved the way to a steady decline of a mass-membership ANC as an organizer of the people, and turned it into a career opening to public sector employment and the administrative "gravy train." It has reduced the tripartite ANC-COSATU-CP alliance from the centrifugal centre of national political mobilization to an electoral pact between parties who are constantly constrained to subordinate their constituents' fundamental interests to the overriding purpose of holding on to administrative power. It has impoverished the soil in which ideas leaning towards socialist solutions once flourished and allowed the weed of "free market" ideology to take hold.[6]

5   Gillian Slovo, *Every Secret Thing* (London: Little-Brown, 1997).

6   Bernstein, R., "Rusty Bernstein: A Letter." in *Transformation*, #64 (2007).

Strong words! To what extent would Ruth have wished to second them herself? Obviously we can never know but the extent that such a question haunts us – or, at least, haunts me – is a measure of how courageous, independent-minded and strong a writer-activist she was, and of how much we all still miss her clear and principled voice.

Nelson Mandela and South Africa's Flawed Freedom[1]

Has the time come when it might be possible to move past the well-deserved praise-song phase of the marking of Nelson Mandela's death in order to strike a more careful balance-sheet on the meaning for present-day South Africa of his storied career?

It remains extremely difficult to speak dispassionately on such matters this close to his impressive funeral, of course. Nor can there be any real debate about the quality of the man or the crucial importance of the role he played, especially in his early years of defiance and in his long, unbending period in prison. Then his courage and his conviction that racist rule, with all its enormities, could not be allowed to stand shone forth.

And yet his latter-day role – as he moved from prison into the Presidency of an ostensibly "new" South Africa – was a much more debatable one. True, in his first moments of freedom in 1990, at the very moment

---

1   This brief text, written to mark Nelson Mandela's death in late 2013 and completed just as the proofs of this book were being finalized for publication, was previously published in the *Toronto Star* (December 16, 2013), at the *Socialist Register* website, and on several South African sites in December, 2013. It seems an appropriate concluding piece to include here, interpreting Mandela's passing, as it does, as the clear herald of a necessary new phase of South and southern Africa's present and future.

that he emerged from captivity, he spoke of the need for multiple "na-tionalizations" and for the injection of genuine social and egalitarian purpose into public life.

Nonetheless, Mandela – never a man of the socio-economic left – soon found his commitment to a radical socio-economic policy shift fading fast. Moreover, in this his position was merely coming into line with that of the ANC's upper echelon as they returned from exile.

For mass popular organizations on the shop floor and in the town-ships had become, in the 1980s, much more central to the struggle against apartheid than any military resistance mounted from exile by the ANC. Increasingly, in fact, what was most feared by the South African business and state establishments was the possible emergence of a "revolutionary force," popular and ever more deeply radicalized, that might spring from any sustained confrontation with the combined oppressions of *both* apartheid and of international capitalism.

Business guru Zac de Beer had once warned defenders of capital's stake in South Africa to guard against precisely this: the danger that "the baby of free enterprise" might be "thrown out with the bathwater of apart-heid"! And, by the mid-1980s, the Brian Mulroneys of the world could also see that apartheid itself – long a profitable partner of capital, with racial oppression helping to keep labour cheap – had became dispensable. Better to move to decapitate a "dangerous" popular movement in order to safeguard the existing pattern of class rule and socio-economic power.

Moreover, such arguments did find willing listeners in those ANC notables who had actually spent their own 1980s informally negotiating with both the South African state and with capital – while promising the latter a very tame transition indeed. And by now Mandela was himself ready to accept a "freedom" that merely embraced a neo-liberal version of South Africa, one in line with global capitalism's own priorities.

Not surprising, then, that very little has changed in the lives of the vast mass of South Africans – a sad anti-climax to the once proud anti-apartheid struggle in South Africa. True, Mulroney himself had, by the end of the 1980s, hesitated – still suspicious that the "freedom-fighters" of the ANC, including Mandela himself, were mere "terrorists." Nonetheless, more savvy guardians of corporate power closer to the scene had grasped the fact that only the cooptation of the ANC into a formal position of power could forestall a revolution.

And this is exactly what now happened. The ANC passed into power, and, as the party of "liberation," proceeded actively both to demobilize the people and to seal a deal with global capital. The predictable result: though the economic gap between black and white has shrunk somewhat (with some blacks becoming very wealthy indeed) the gap between rich and poor (still mainly black) has widened dramatically. Crime rates have risen as a reflex of the gross, class-defined imbalance in personal incomes, while among Mandela's successors – Zuma and his cronies – corruption flourishes.

More promisingly, of course, there are also signs of more militant resistance. It is true that a genuinely effective and credible counter-hegemonic national alternative to the ANC has been slow to emerge. But the extent of social protest against the state – demonstrations, protests and other forms of social disobedience – that is evident at the local level is now higher than anywhere else in the world!

Here too may also lie the silver lining in Mandela's own passing from the scene. For, after an initial and fully understandable period of general mourning, the removal from the ANC of the brilliant lustre of Madiba's public image and the halo of his almost supra-historical resonance might mean a further diminishing of the once seemingly impregnable image that the ANC, at least at the national level, has managed to sustain. If so, a further beneficial levelling of the playing field of political contestation would occur and, after Mandela, the struggle for a more meaningful liberation could further intensify in South Africa.

Index

workers: interests of, 153; protests by in Mozambique, 58–59; protests by in South
    Africa, 65; rights of in Mozambique, 49–50
working class, 13, 100, 106, 109; agency defined in terms of, 114; ambiguities of,
    101–8; availability of self-defense organizations, 104; belonging, 117;
    concentration and centralization of, 103; conceptual boundaries of action
    of, 104; consciousness, 108; in Mozambique, 49; and poor, 162; protest
    by, 107; radicalized, 132; resistance of in South Africa, 65–71, 115; revo-
    lutionary agency of, 100; struggles of, 107
workplace protest, 106–8, 112, 116–17, 137
World Bank, 6, 46, 54, 126
World Social Forum, 12n14
World Summit on Social Development, 147
World Wars, 123
Wright, Phil, 110–11

xenophobia, 76, 104, 118, 167

York, Geoffrey, 10–11, 159
Younis, Mona, 76–77

Zambia, 35, 45
Zanzibar, 29. *See also* Tanzania
Zelig, Leo, 171
Zimbabwe, 11, 23, 27, 144, 167; independence of, 20; liberation struggles in, 2;
    Movement for Democratic Change (MDC), 26, 144; regional struggle in,
    121; treatment of by South Africa, 24–25. *See also* Rhodesia
Zimbabwe African National Union (ZANU), 23
Zuma, Jacob, 94n63, 152